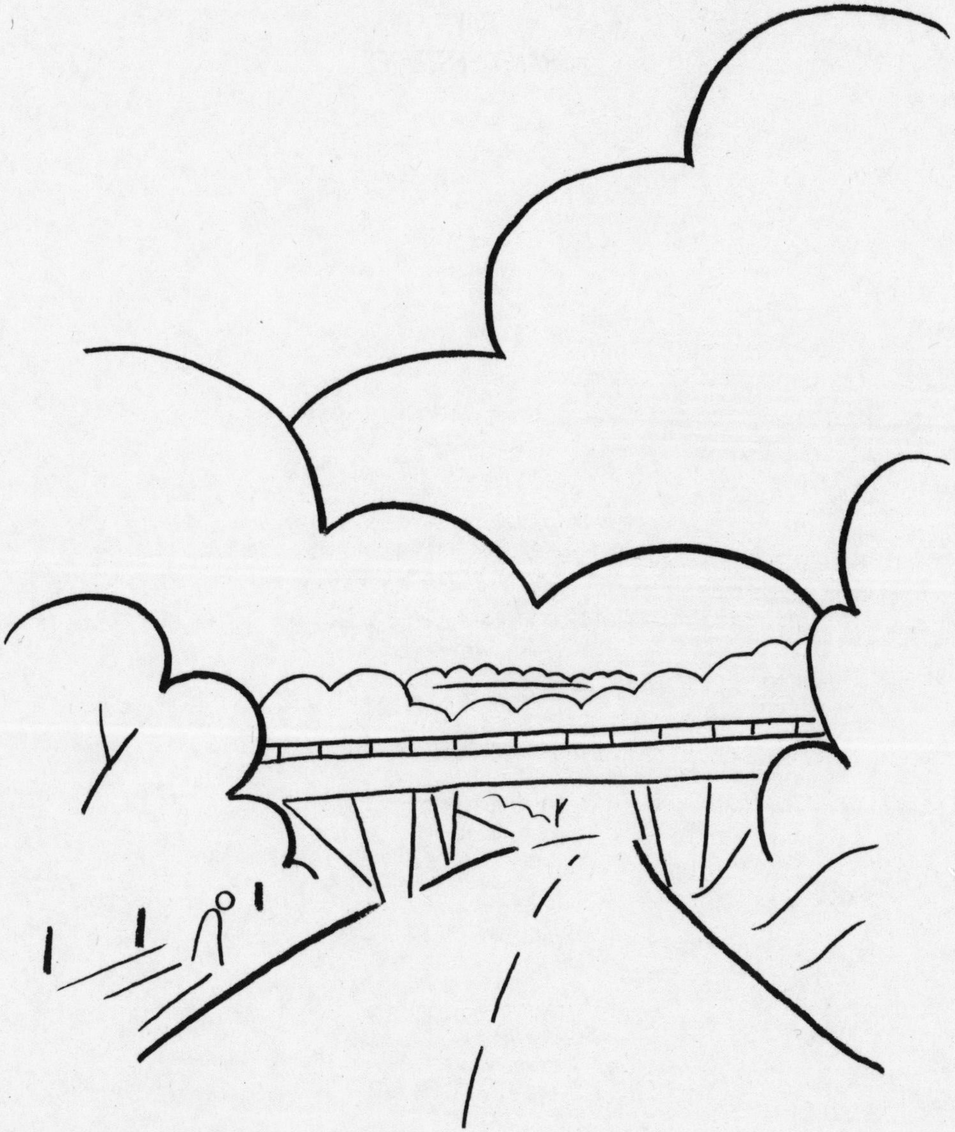

Also by Simon Moreton:

DAYS
GRAND GESTURES

Art Direction by Tom Kaczynski and Simon Moreton
Production and Design by Jordan Shiveley

UNCIVILIZED BOOKS
P. O. Box 6534
Minneapolis, MN 55406
USA
uncivilizedbooks.com

First Edition, October 2015

10 9 8 7 6 5 4 3 2 1

ISBN 978-1-941250-06-8

DISTRIBUTED TO THE TRADE BY:
Consortium Book Sales & Distribution, LLC.
34 Thirteenth Avenue NE, Suite 101
Minneapolis, MN 55413-1007
cbsd.com
Orders: (800) 283-3572

Printed in Canada

PLANS WE MADE
SIMON MORETON

UNCIVILIZED BOOKS

EARLY ON

WE USED TO MEET AT THE POSTBOX
BY THE CORNERSHOP

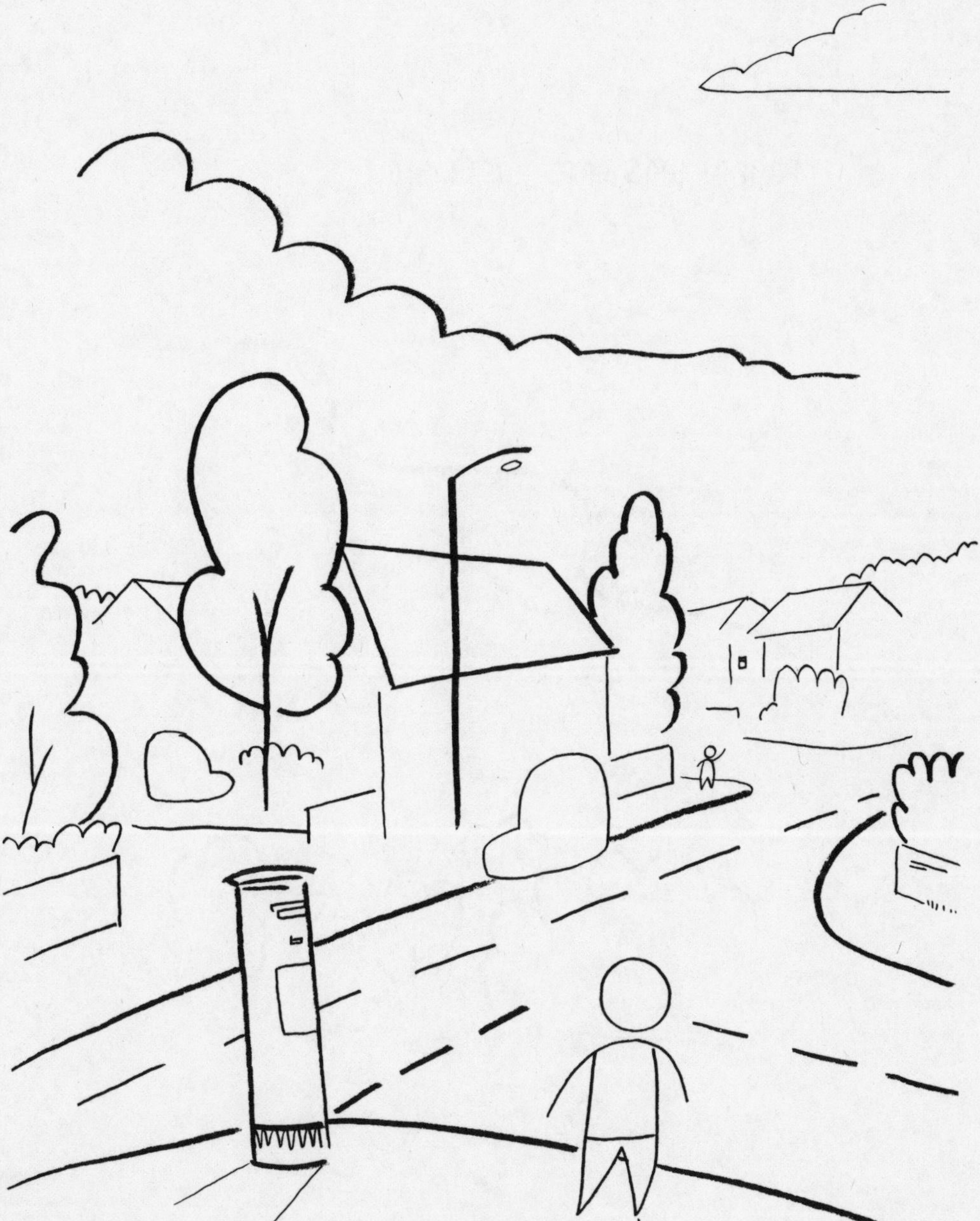

HAYDN WAS LATE EVERY TIME

ENDLESS SUMMERS

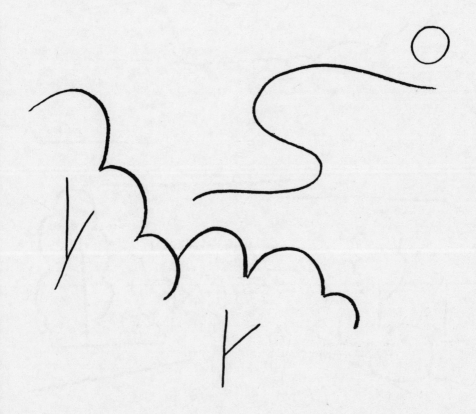

THE EVENINGS WHEN IT WAS HOT

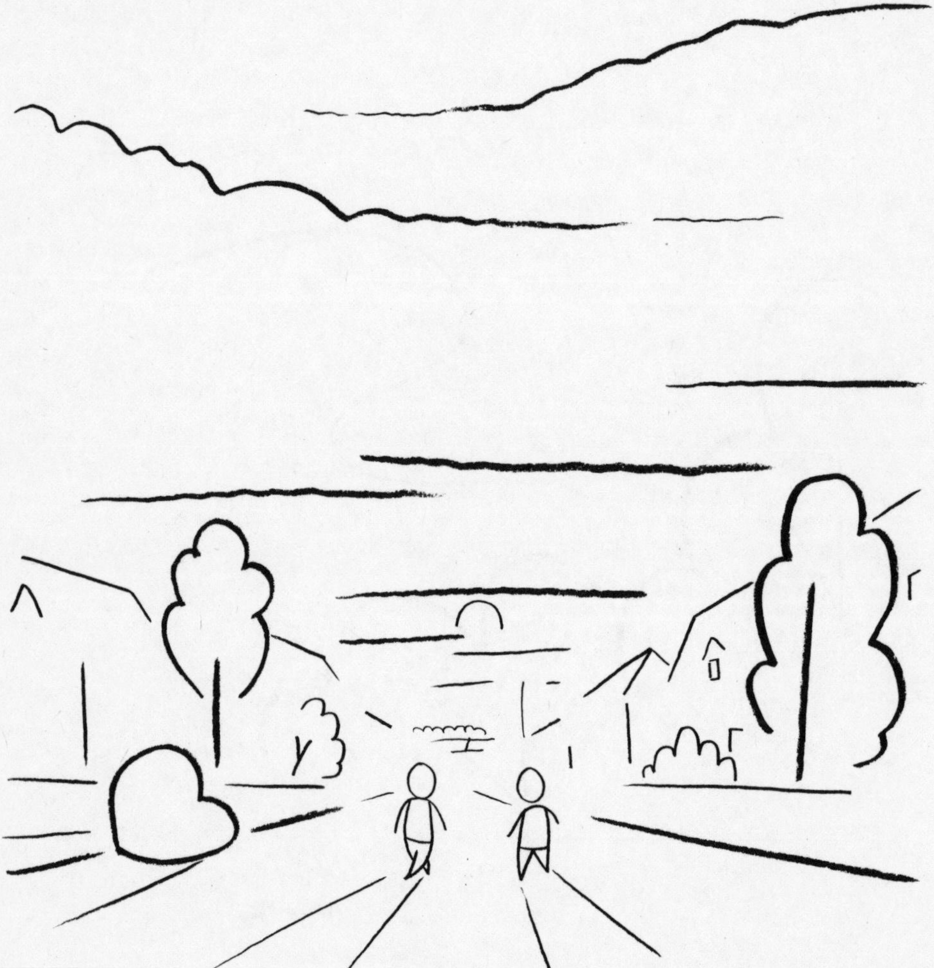

AND THE TARMAC STUCK TO OUR SHOES

THE HOUSES PEOPLE WERE PROUD OF

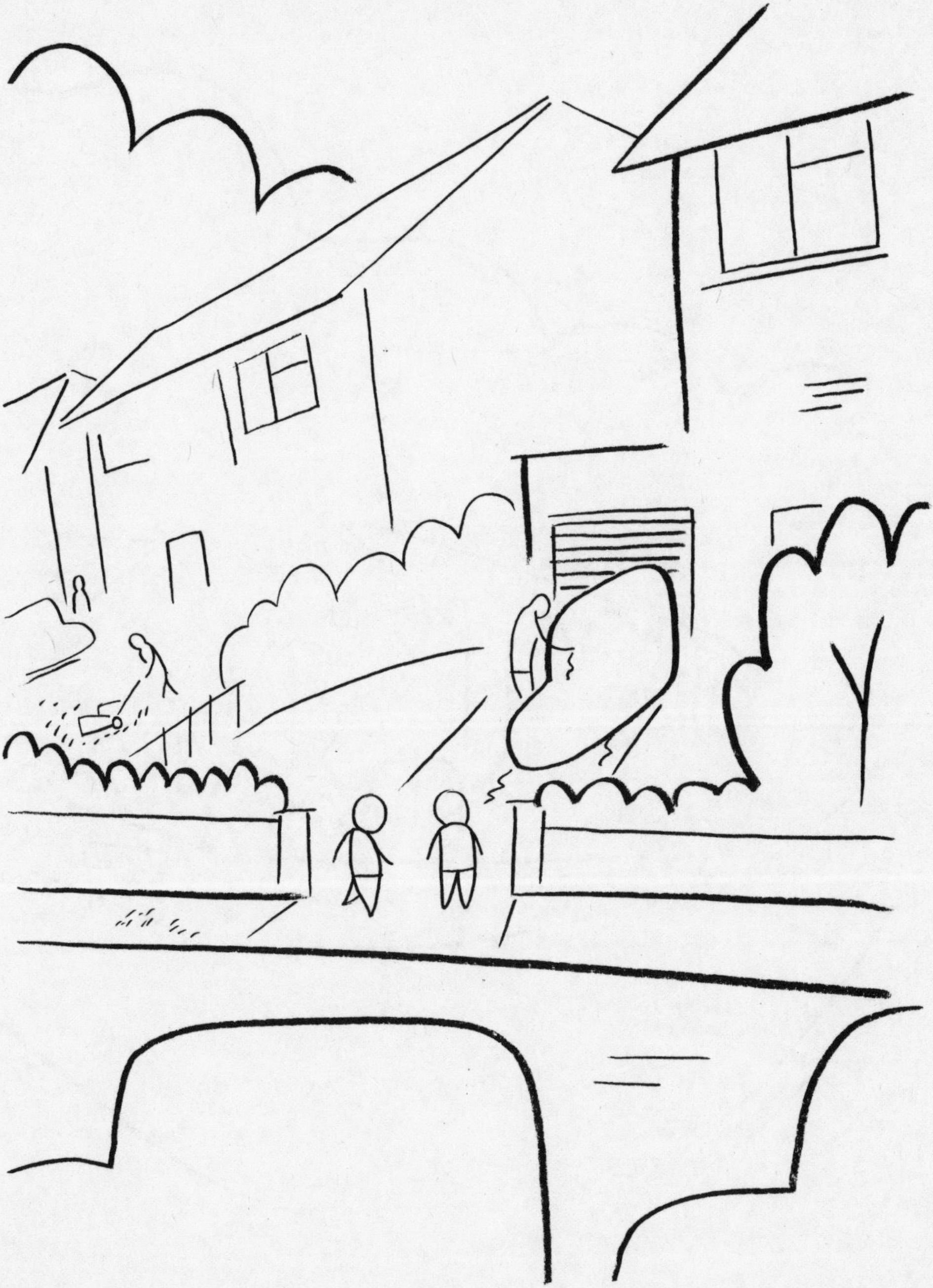

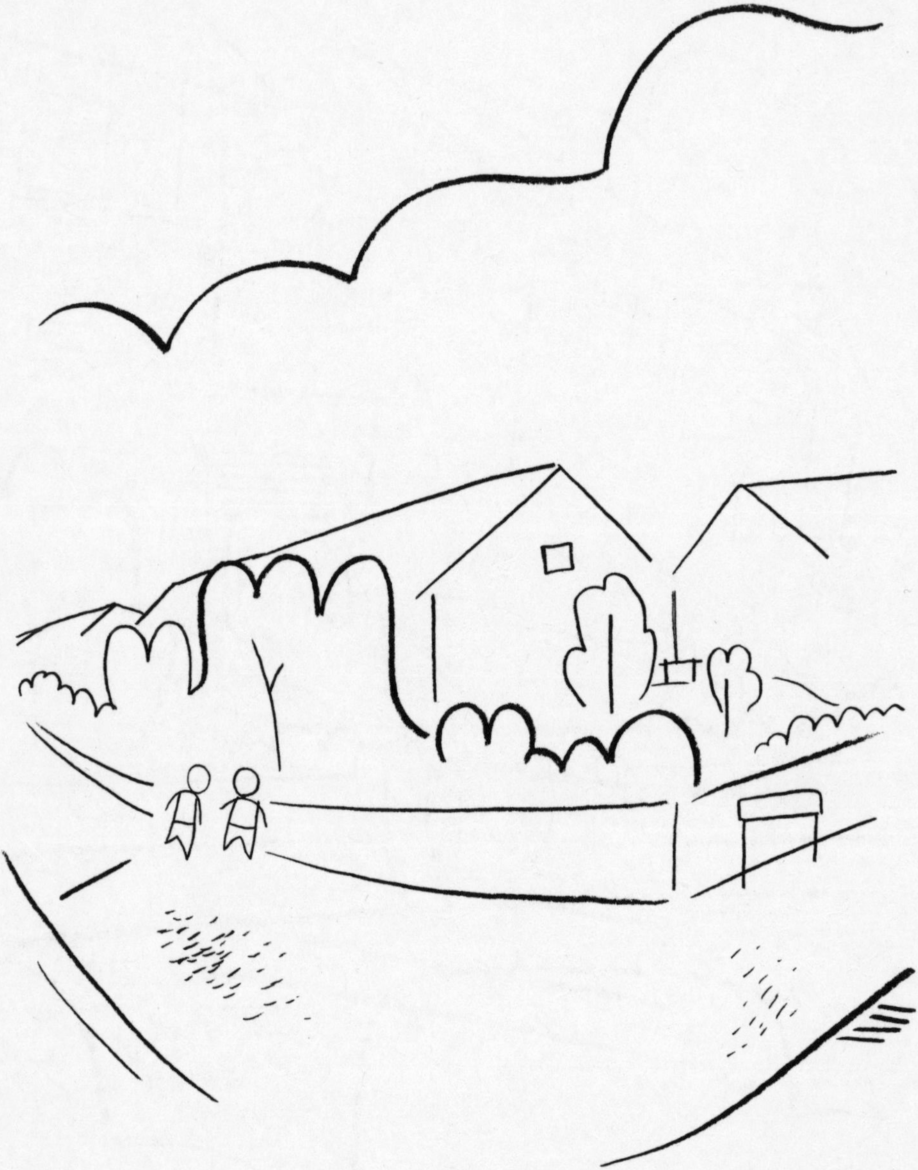

THE BLEACHED GRASS VERGES

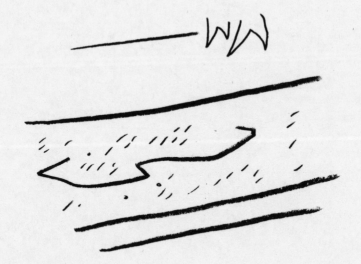

I HAD A SLEEPOVER FOR MY TWELFTH BIRTHDAY

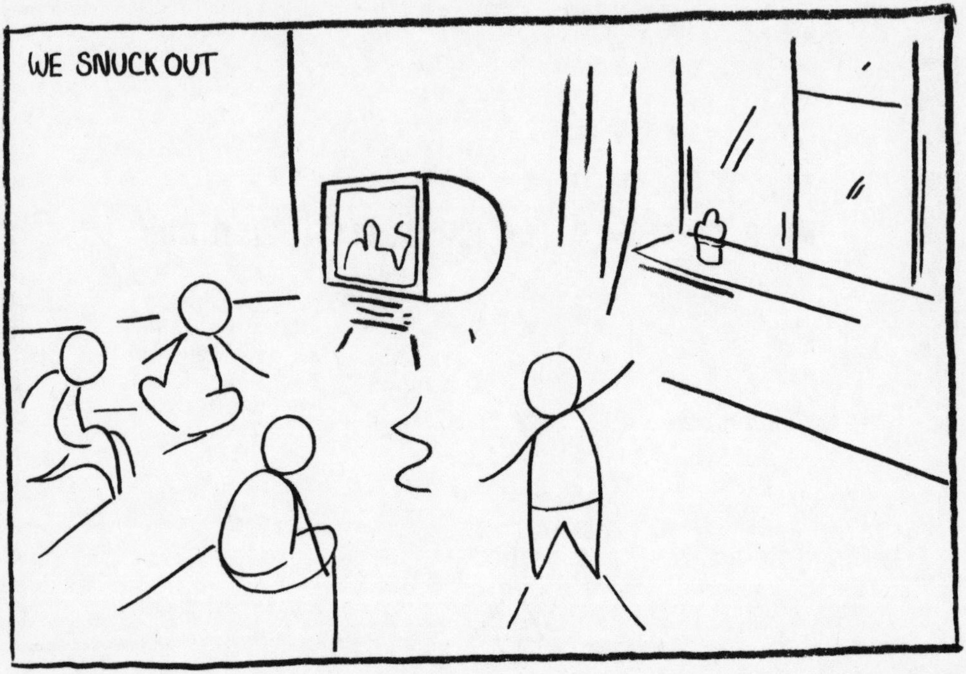
WE SNUCK OUT

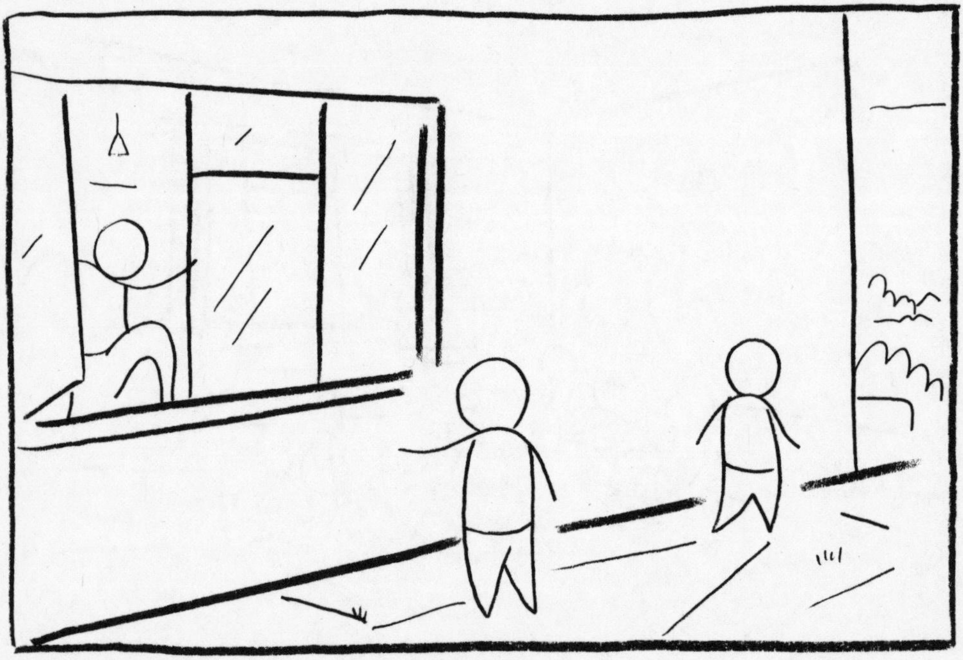

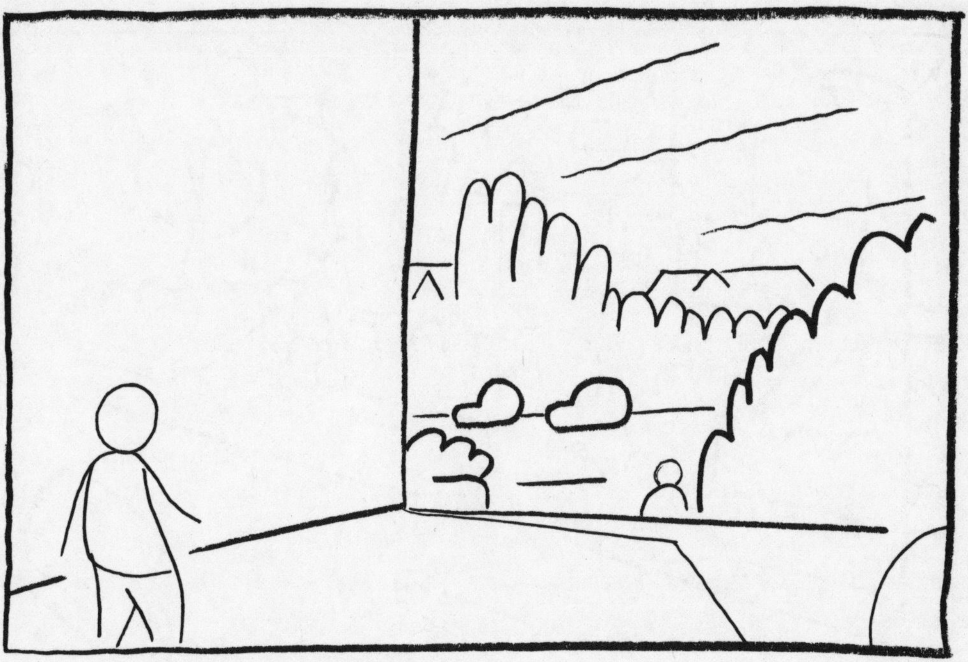

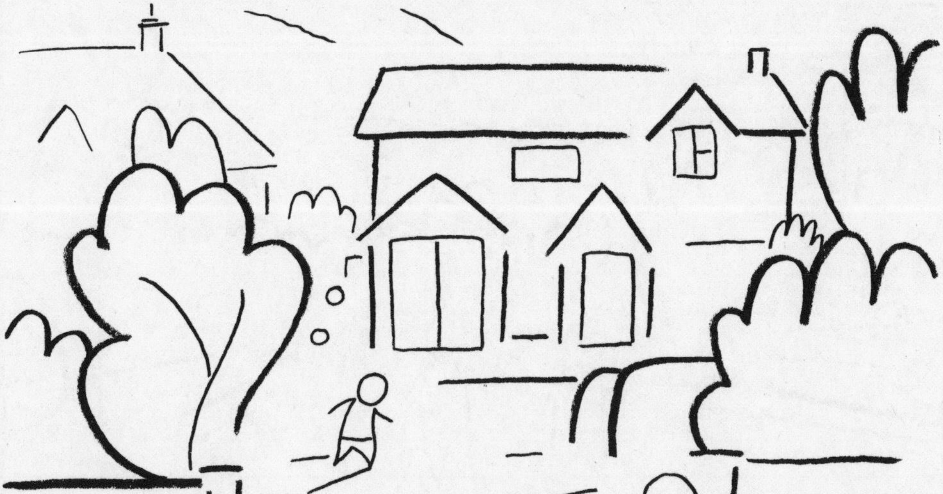

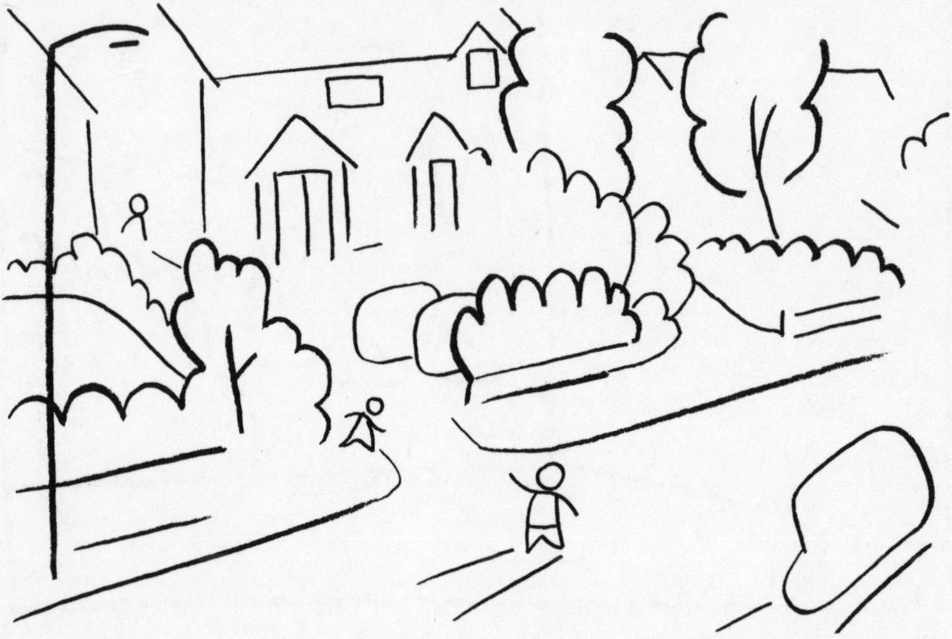

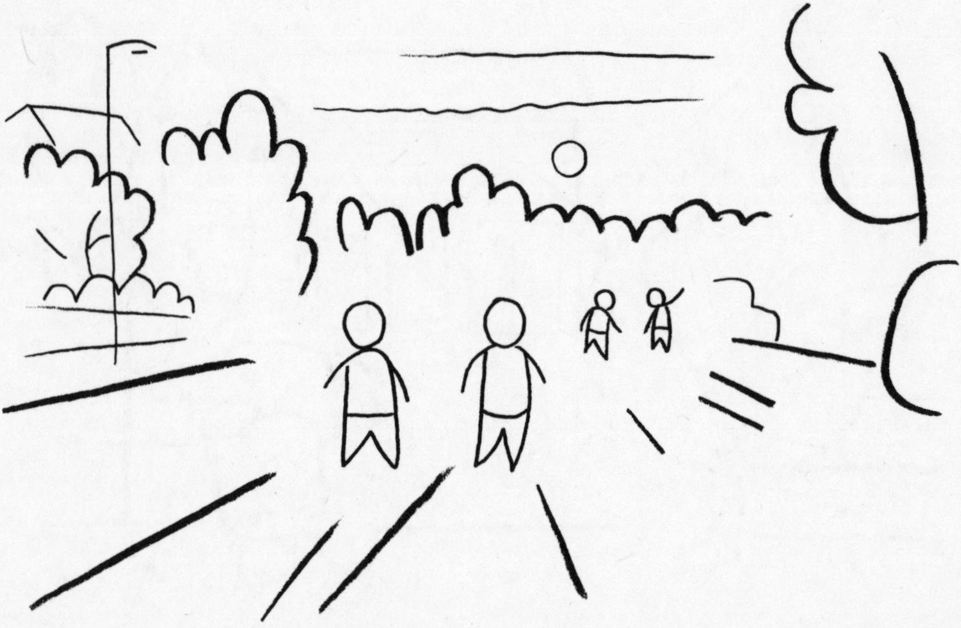

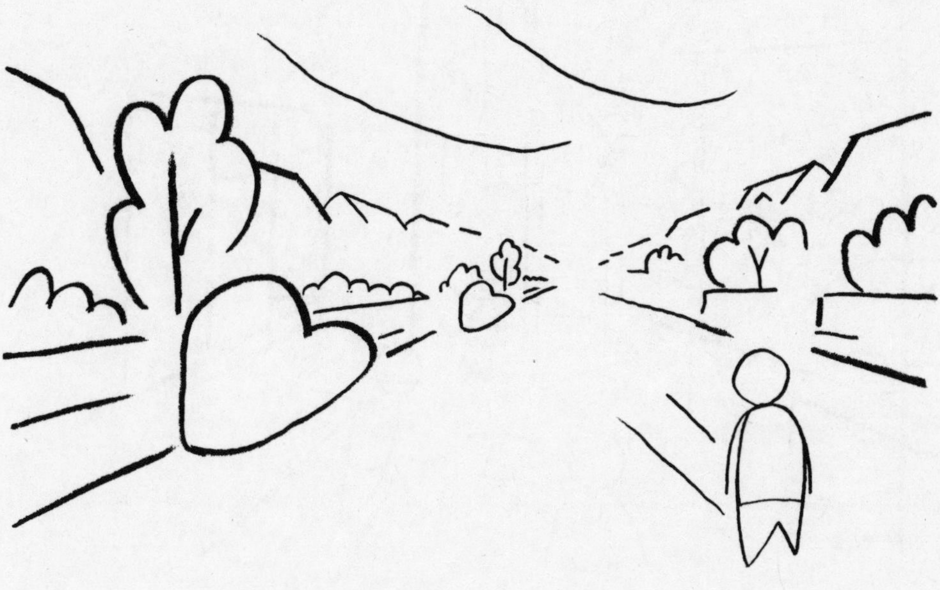

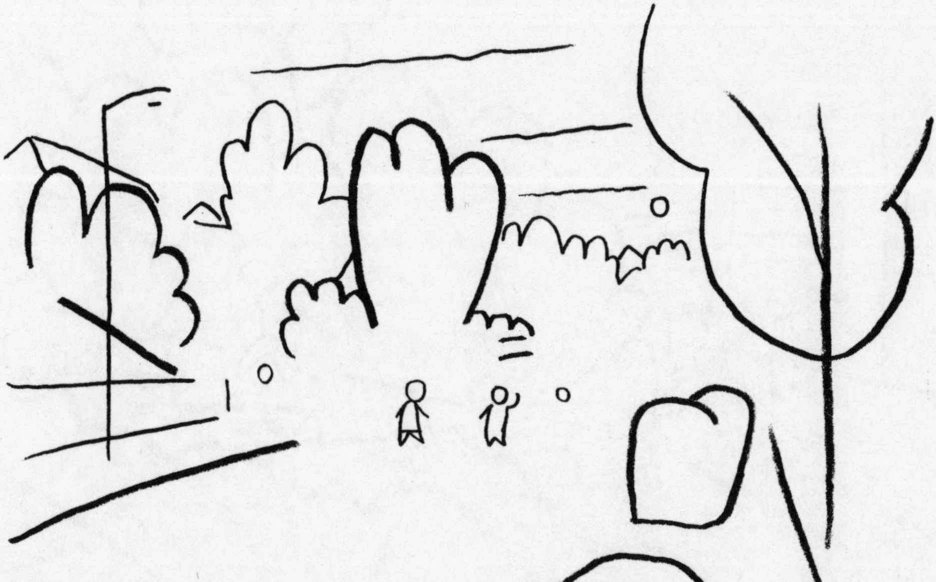

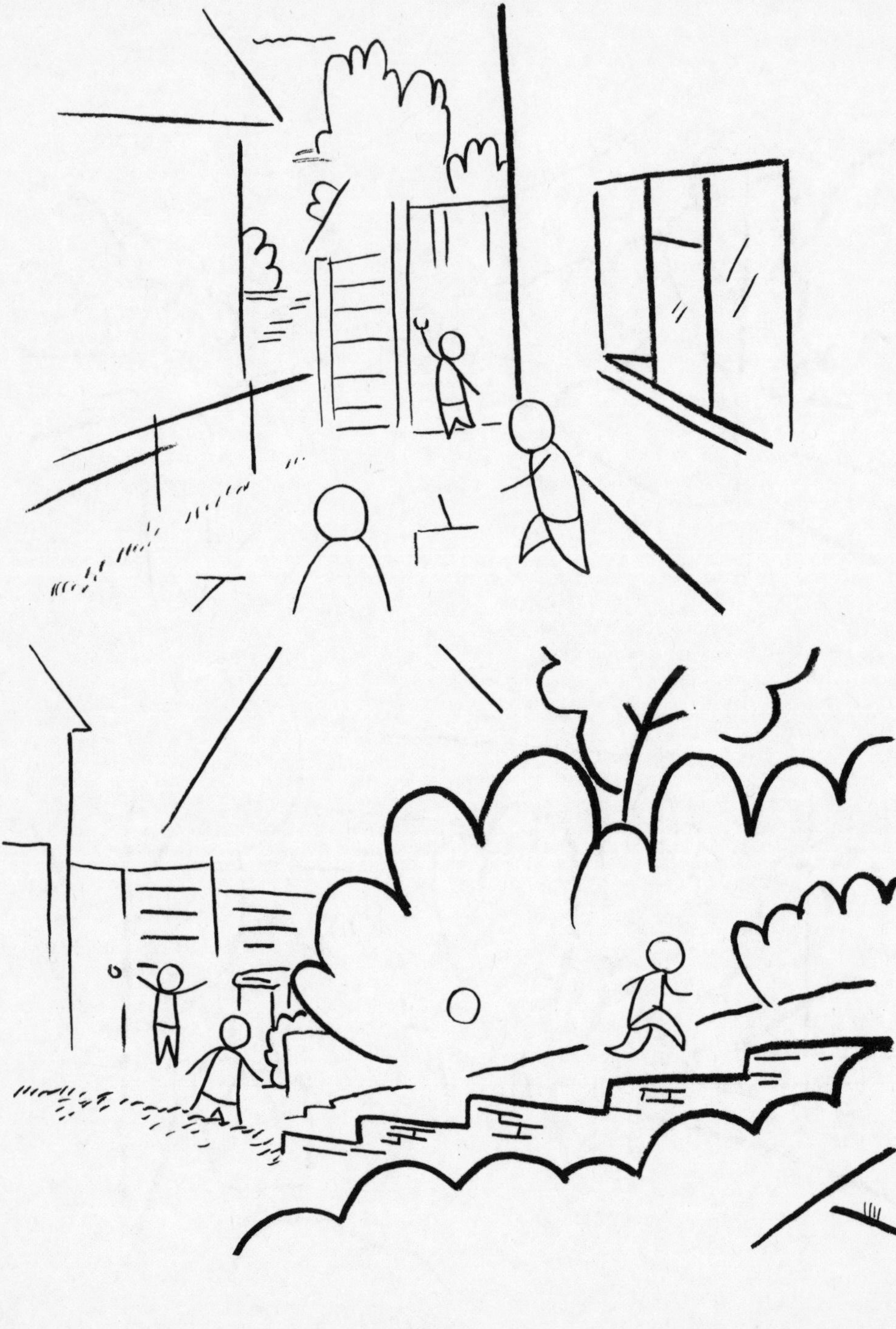

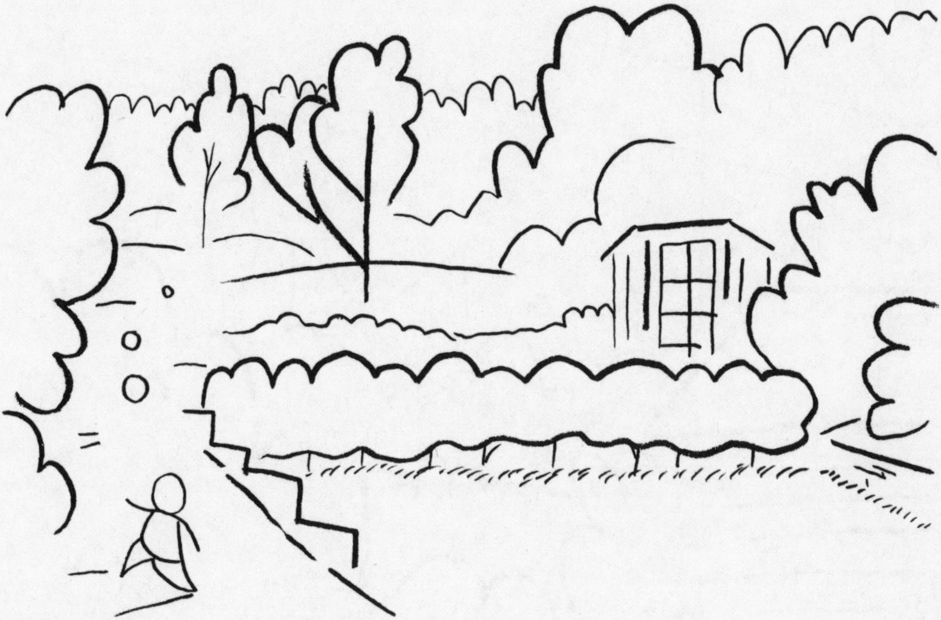

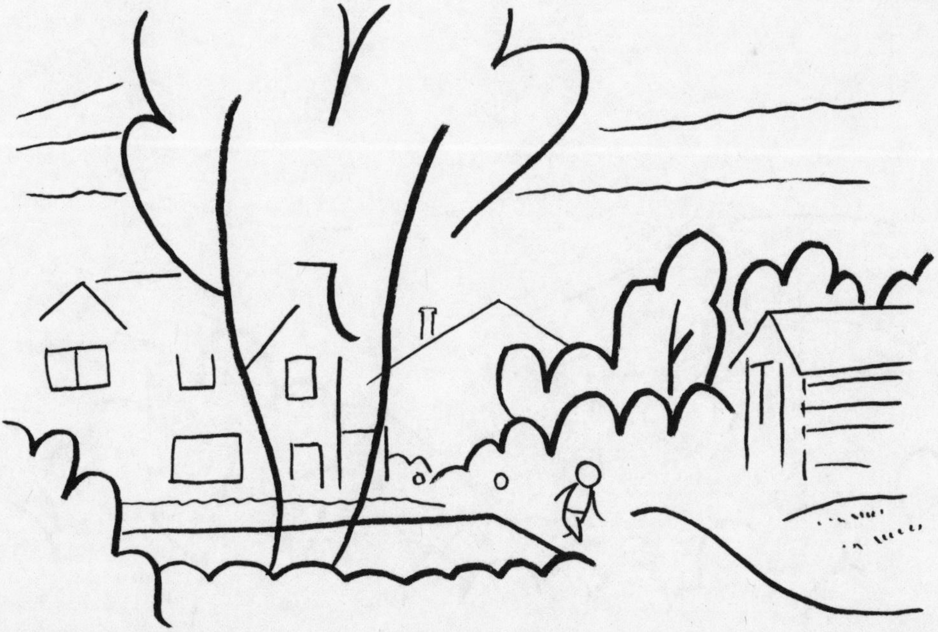

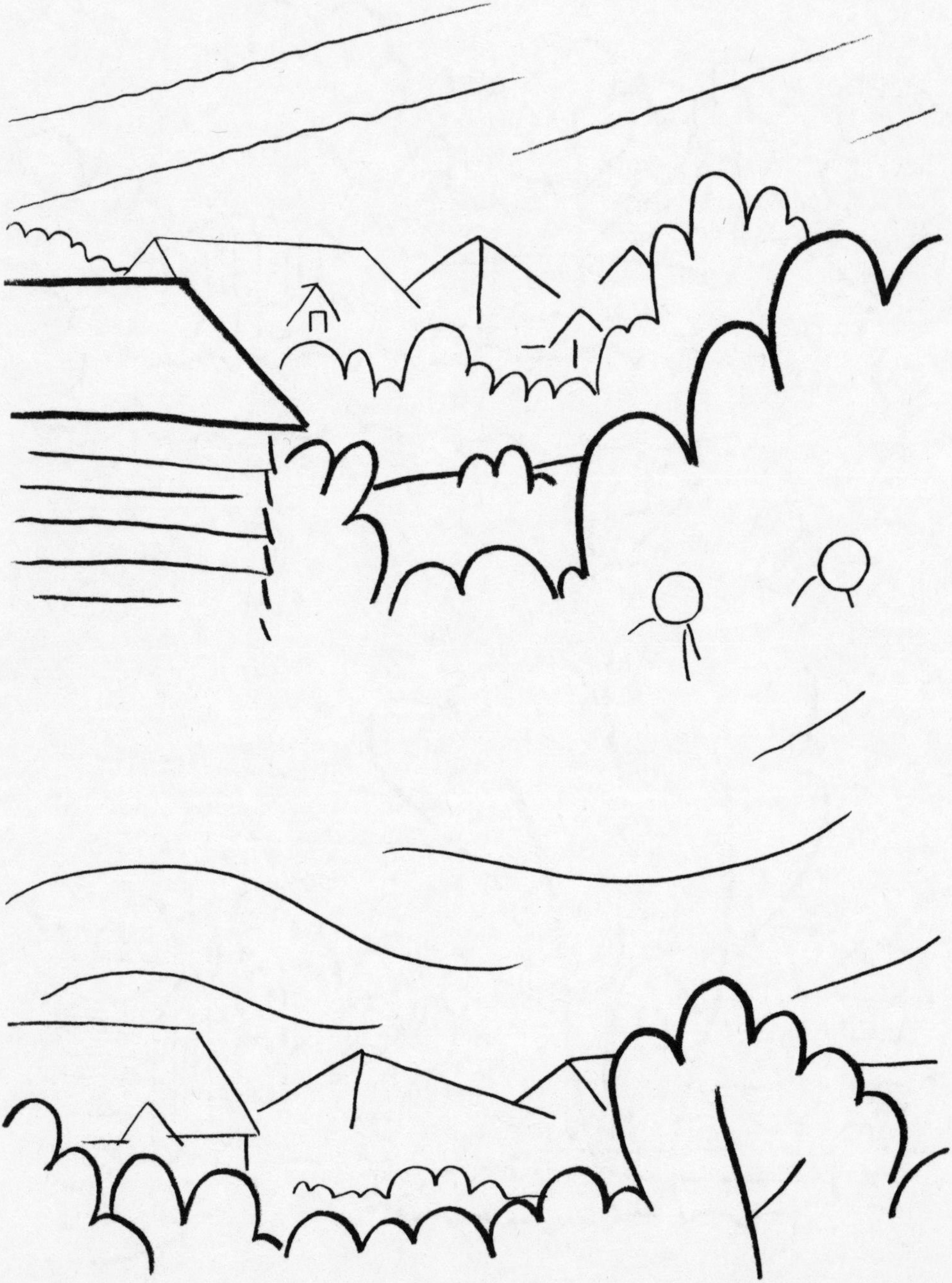

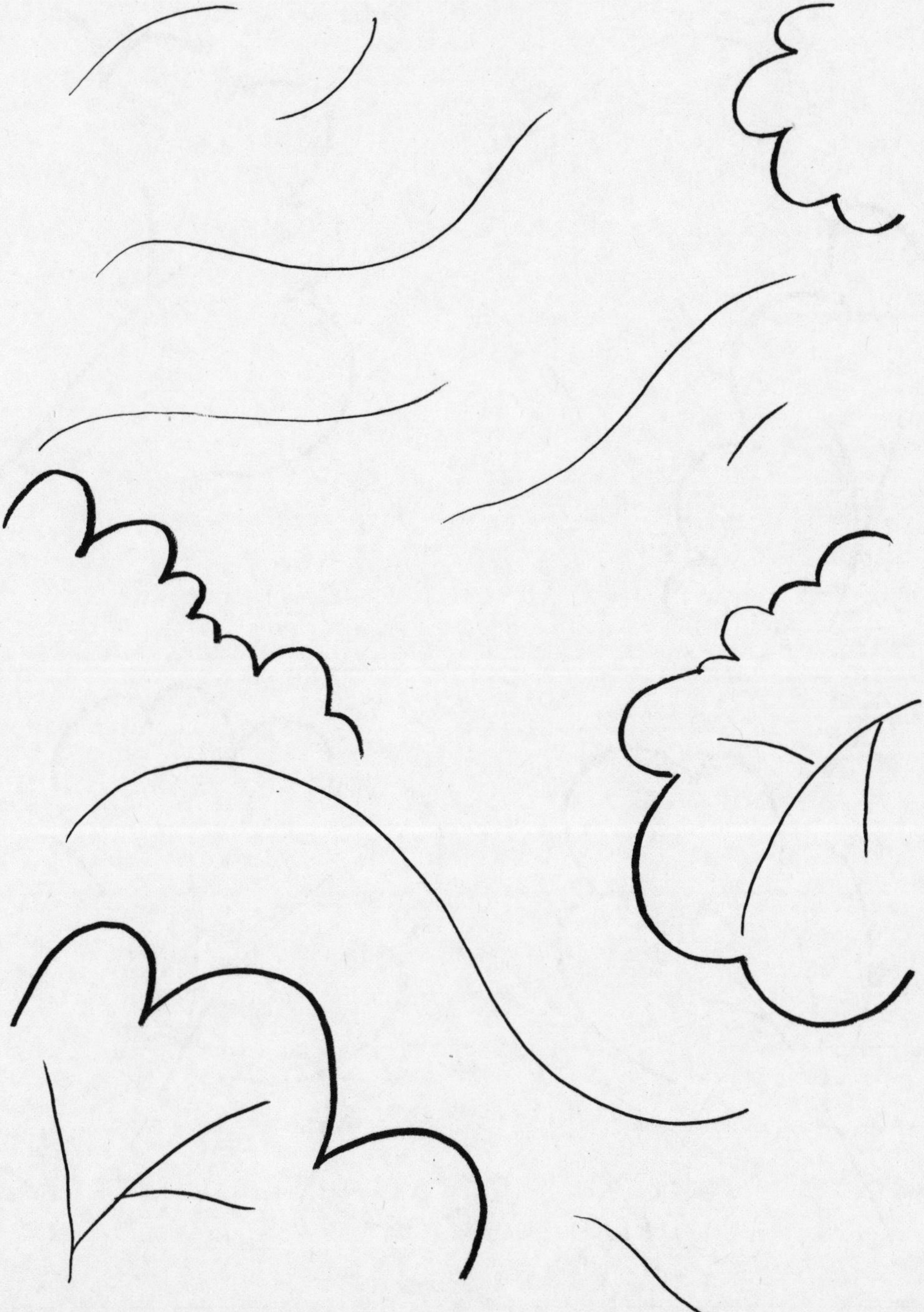

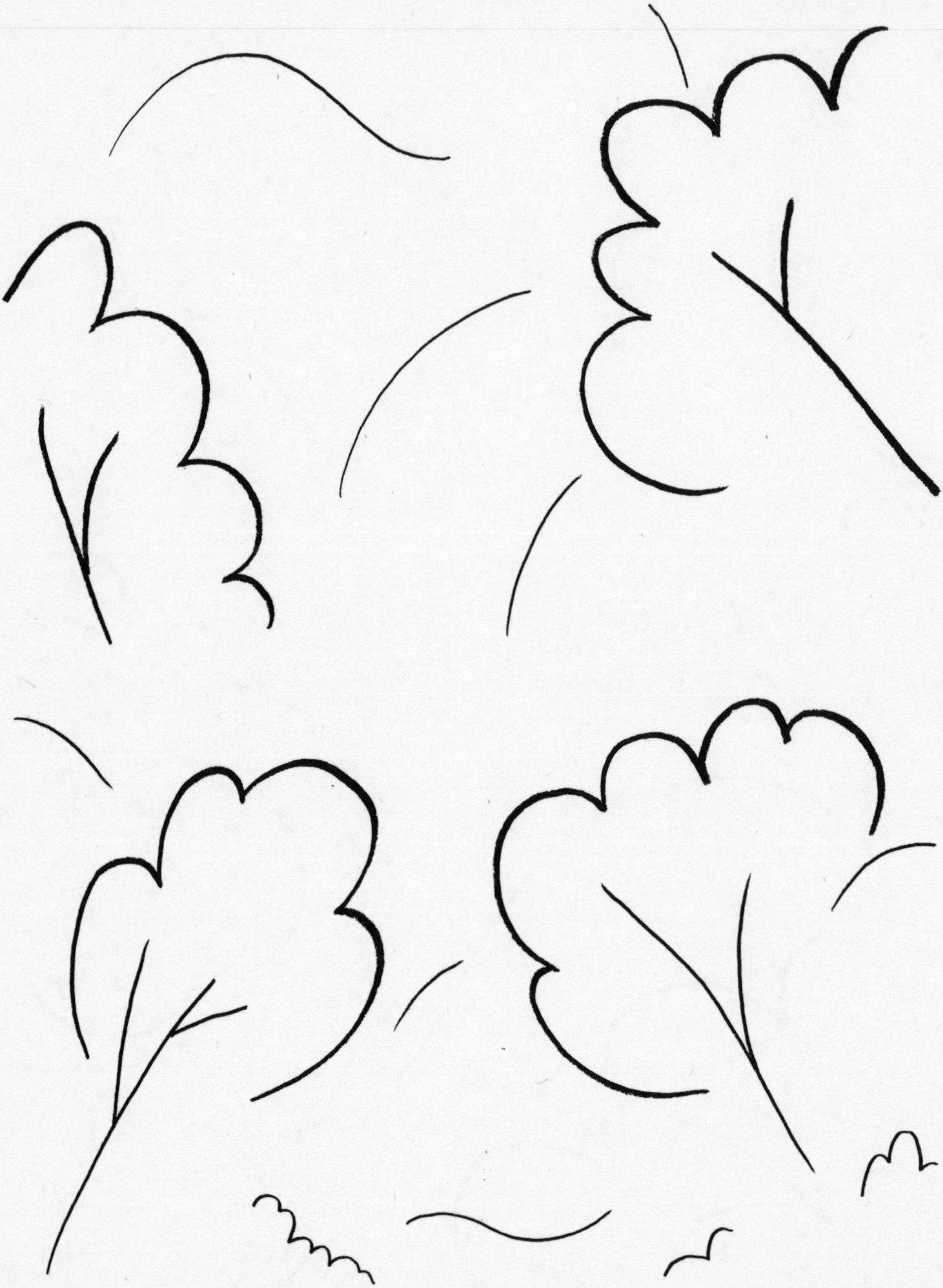

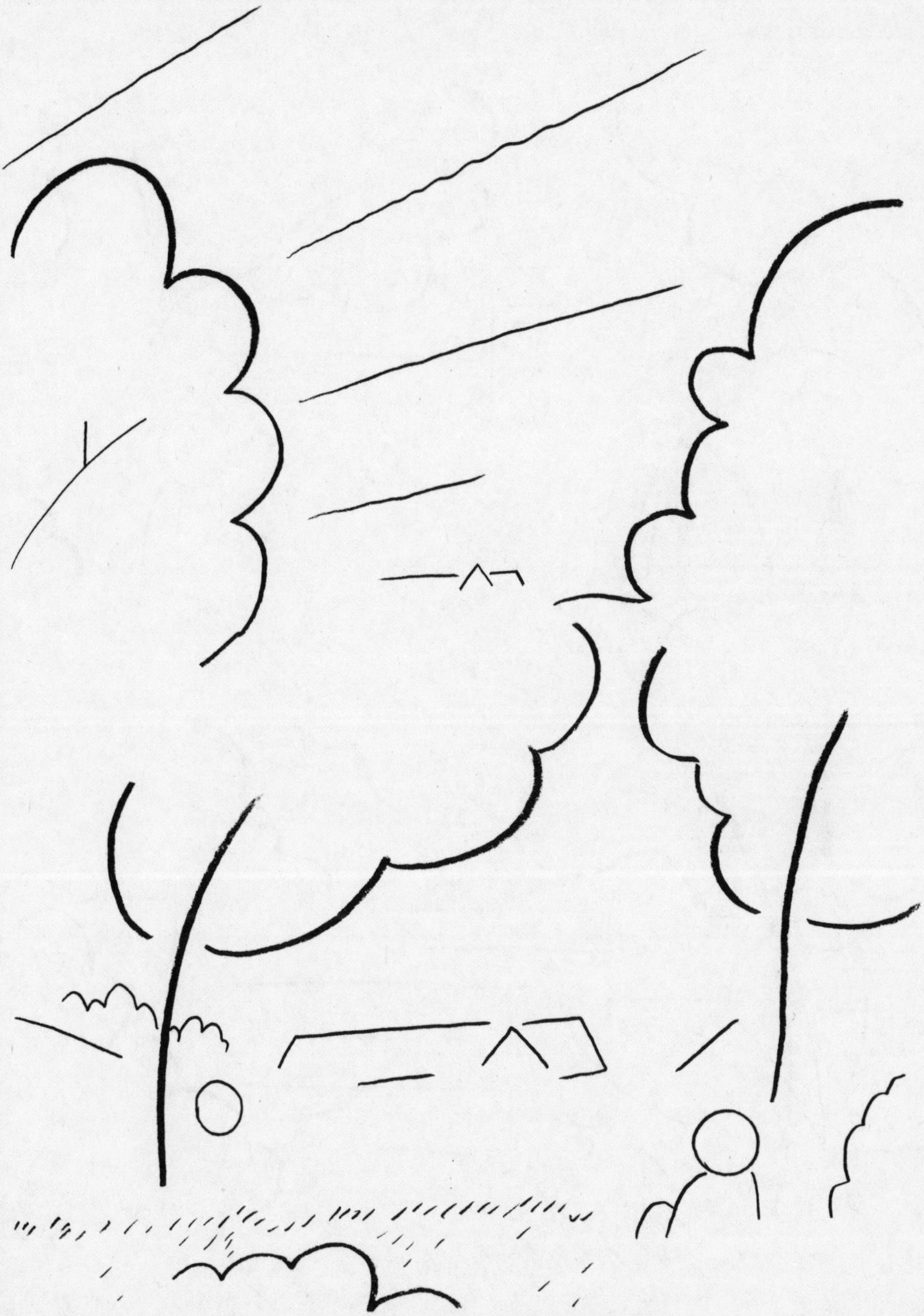

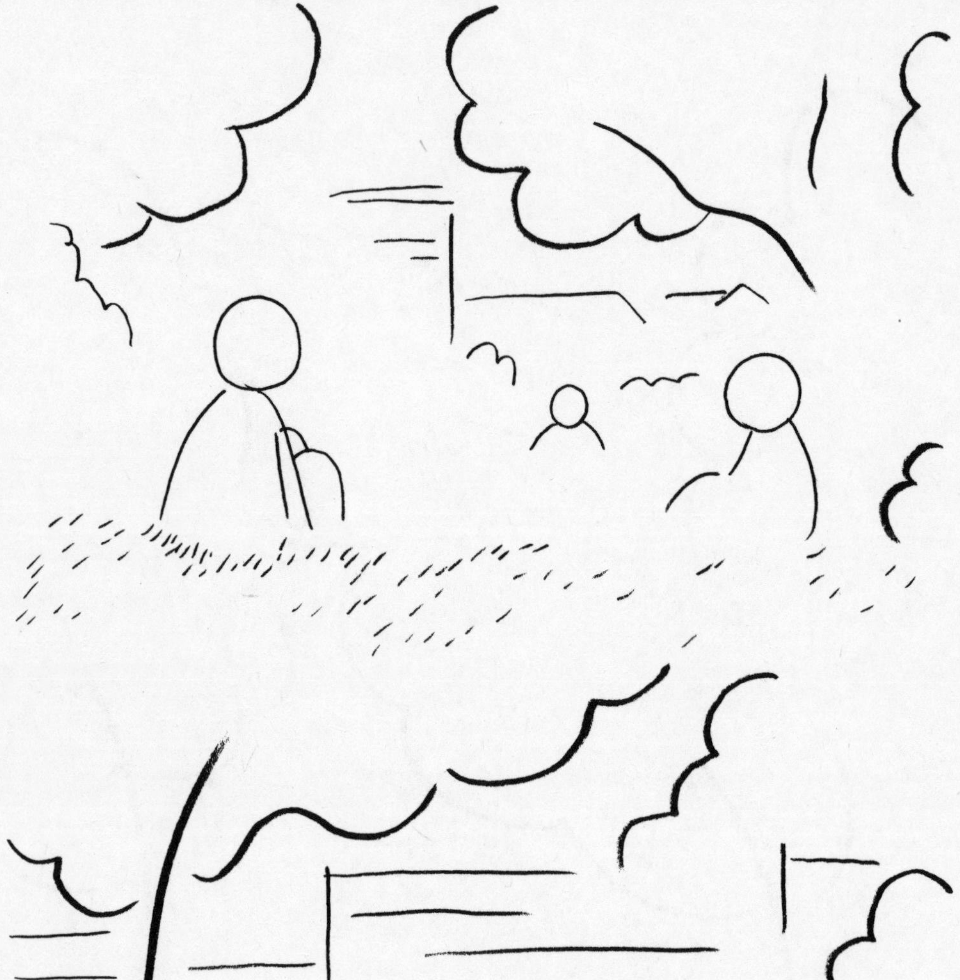

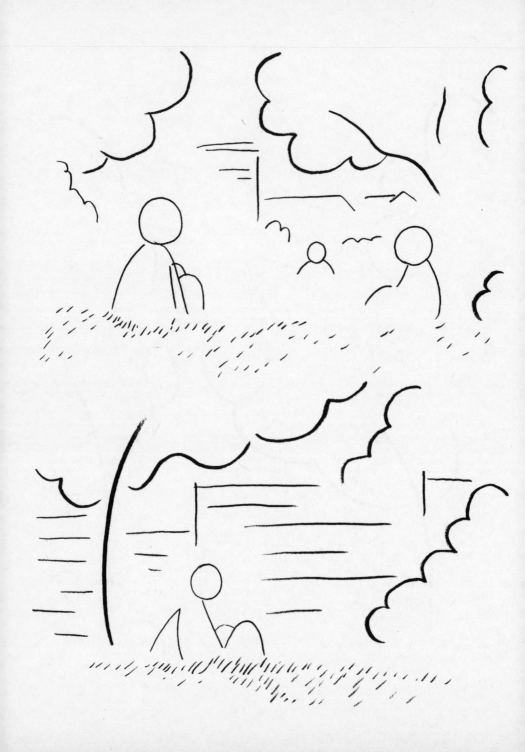

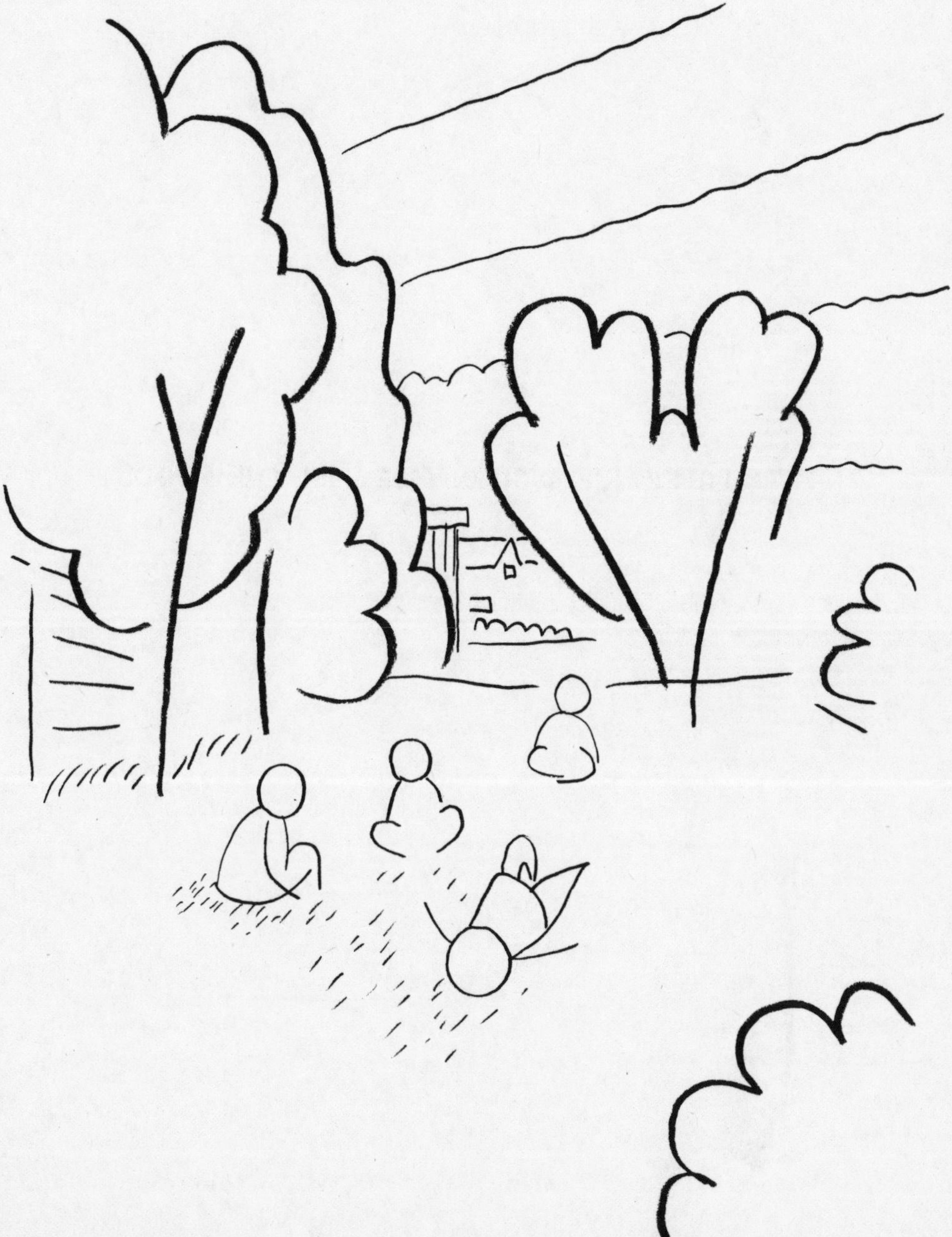

LATER WE WOULD MEET IN THE WOODS

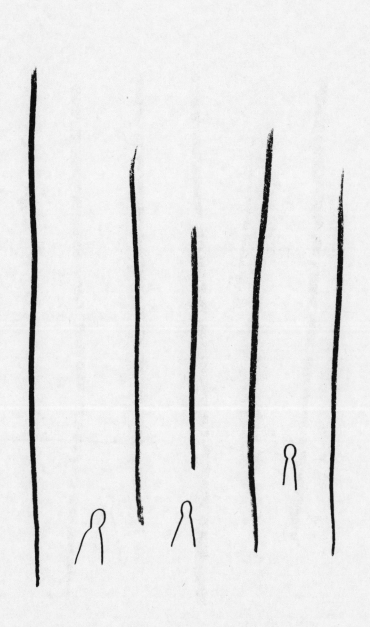

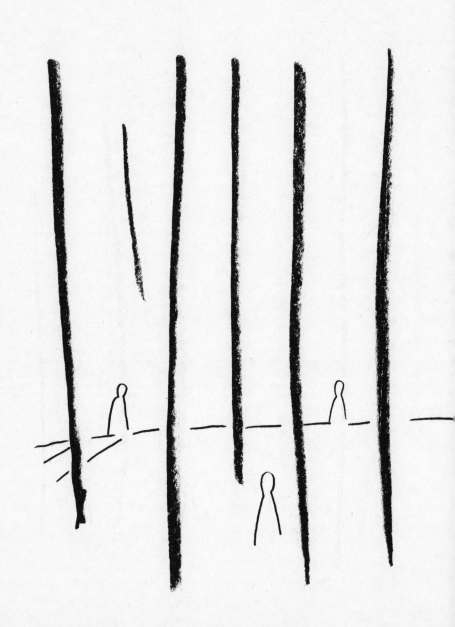

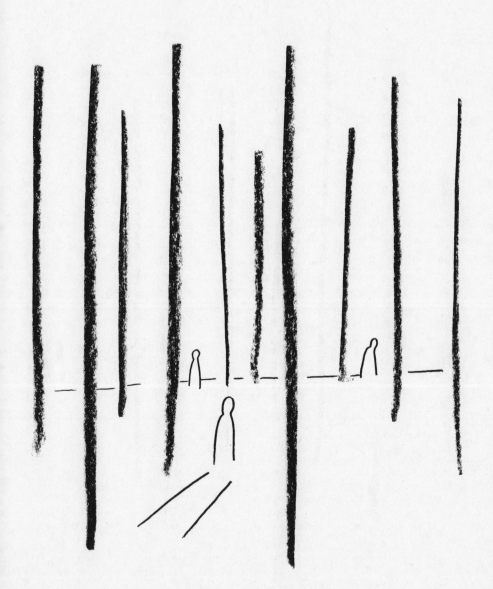

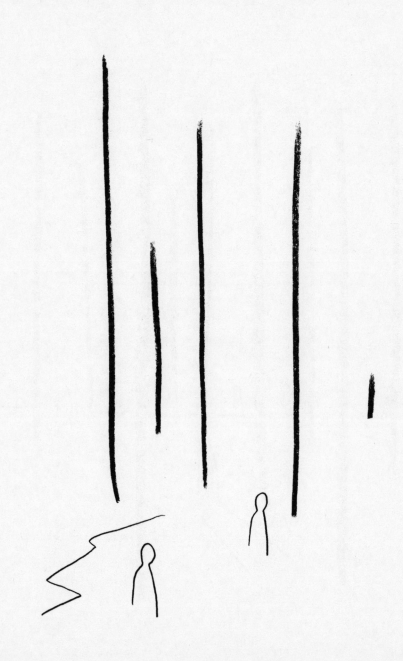

AND NOTICE ONE ANOTHER FOR THE FIRST TIME

IT'S THE LITTLE MOMENTS I REMEMBER

LIKE A LIFT HOME
WITH HAYDN'S OLDER NEIGHBOUR

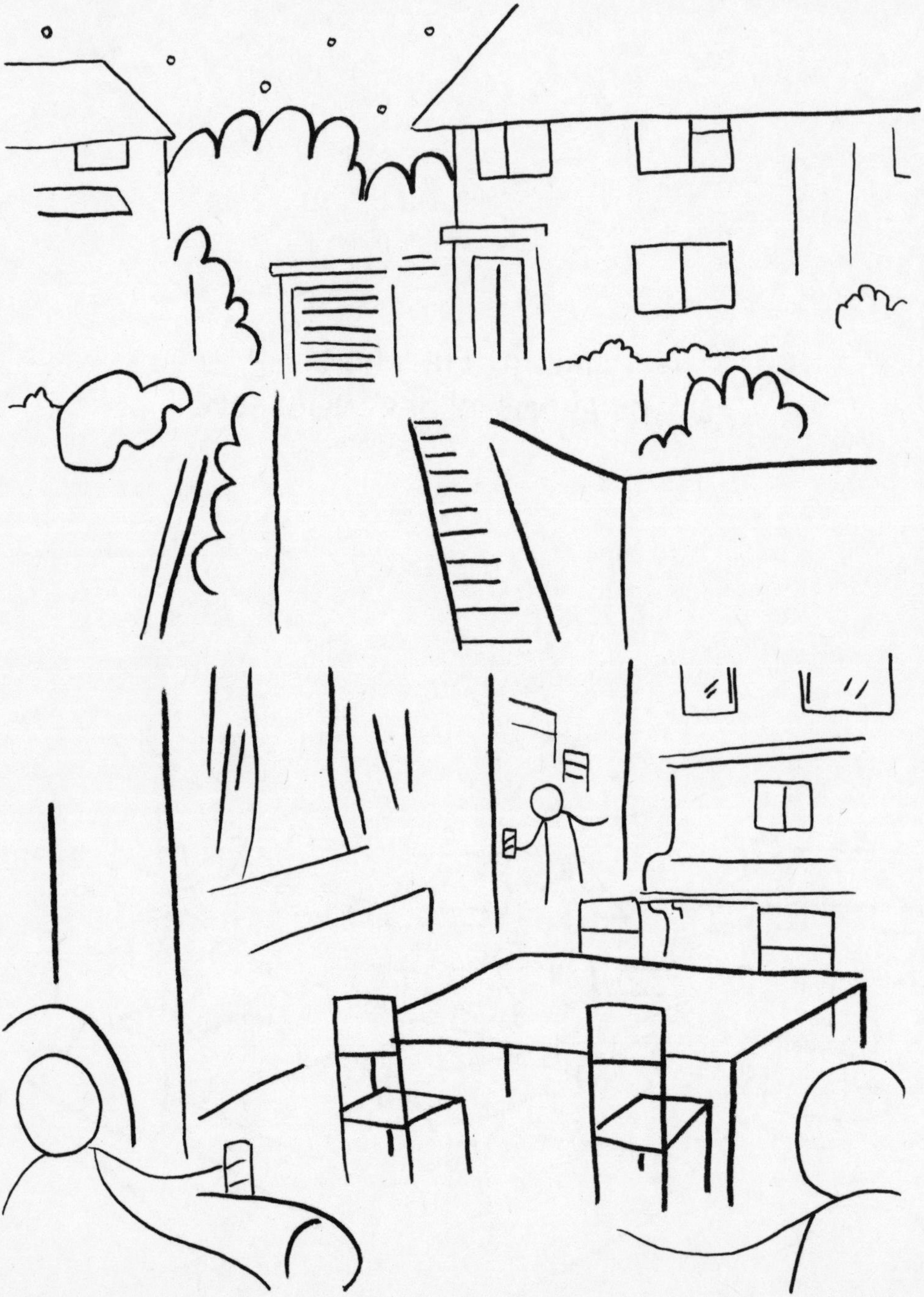

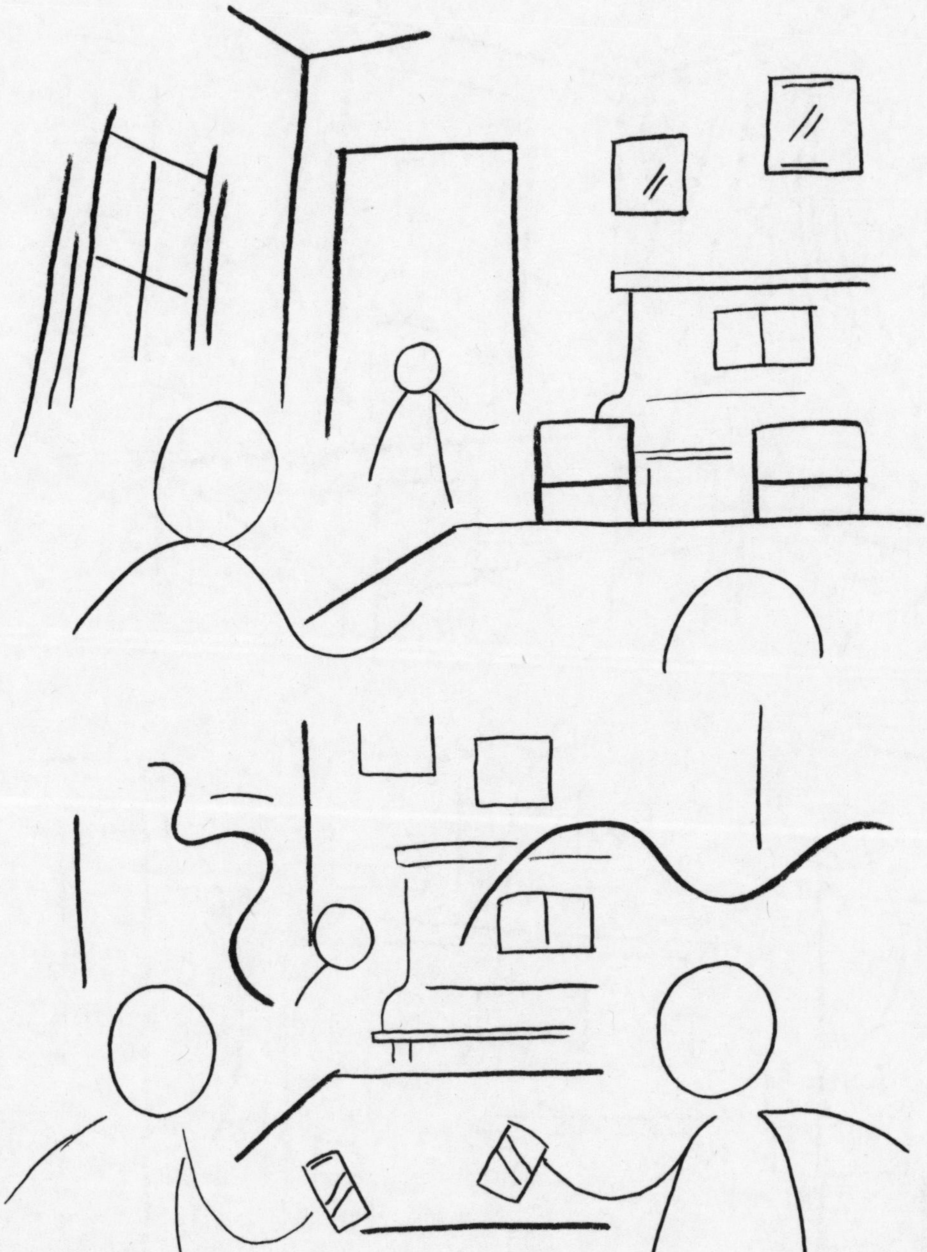

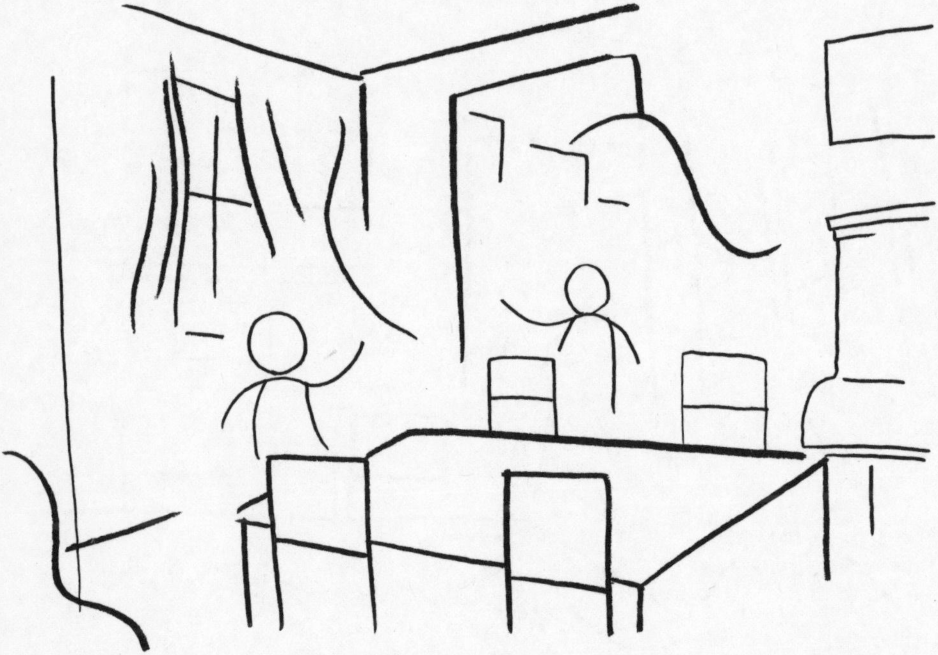

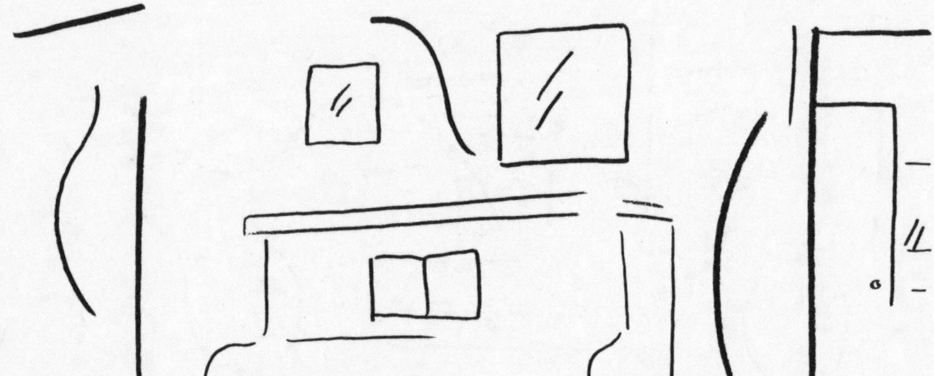

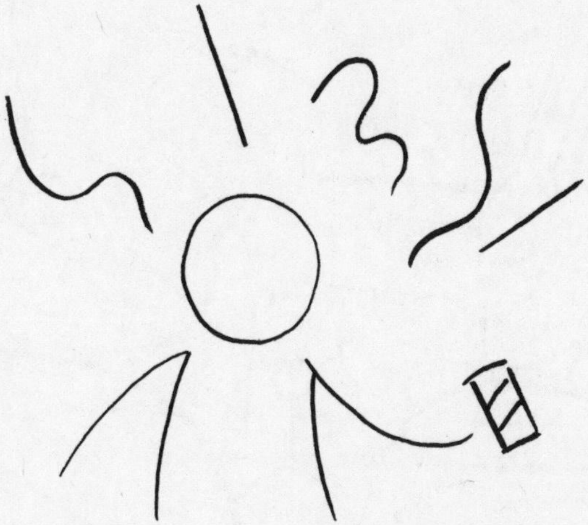

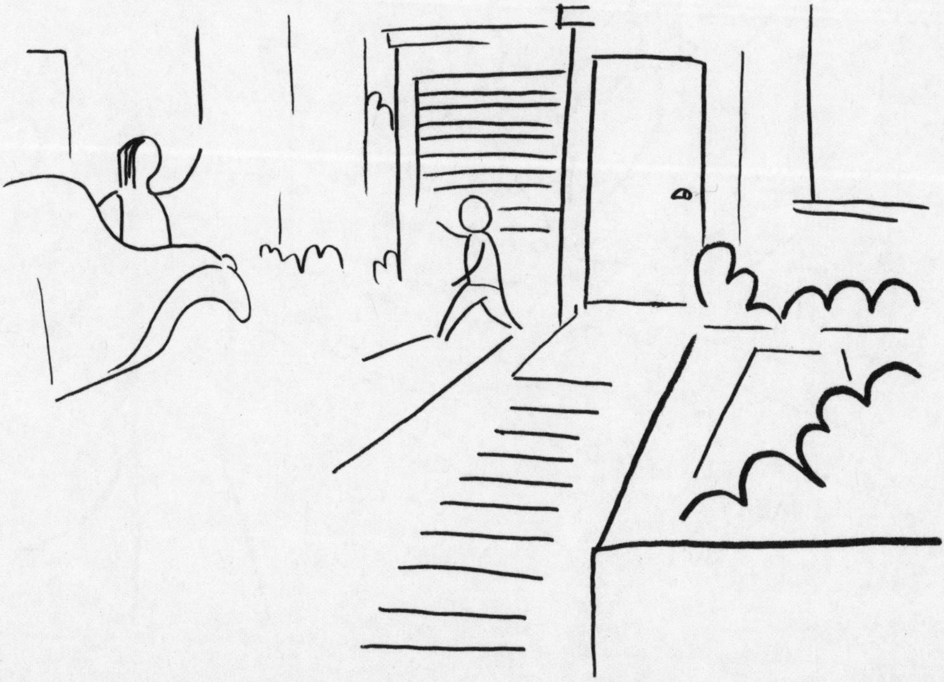

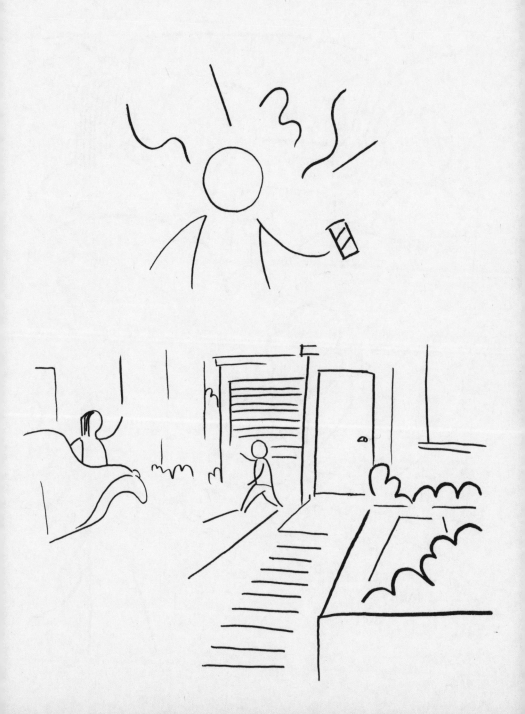

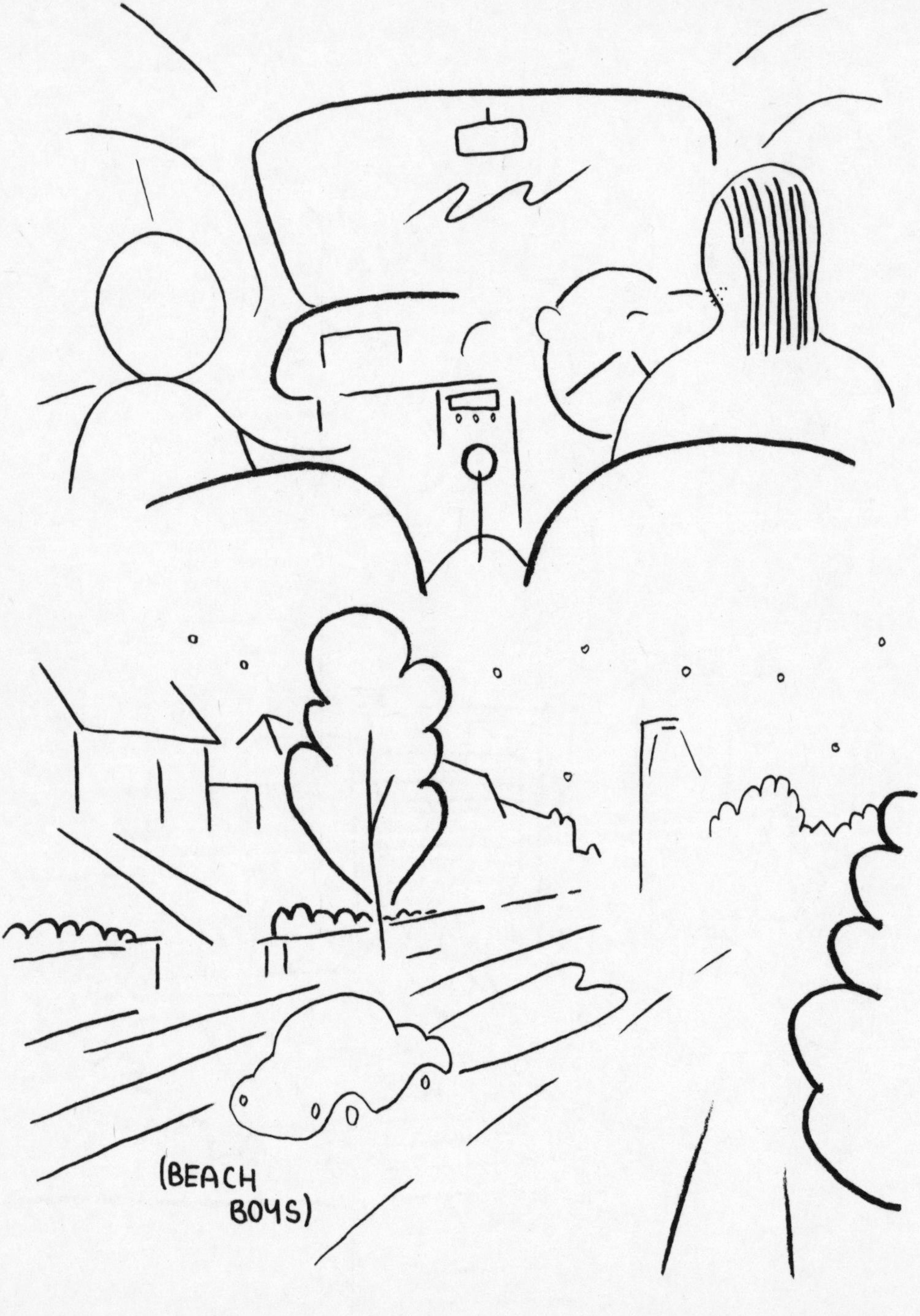
(BEACH
BOYS)

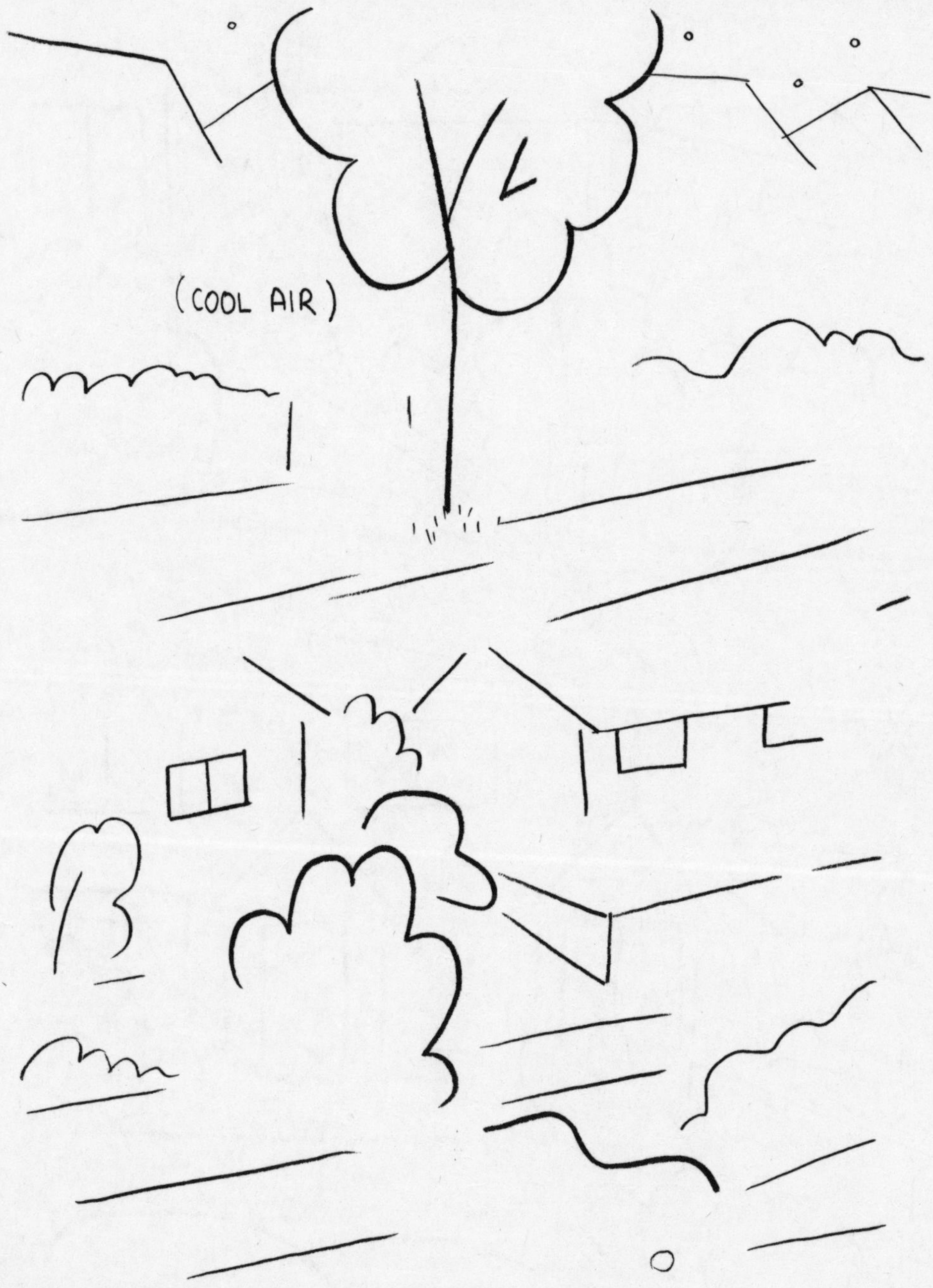
(COOL AIR)

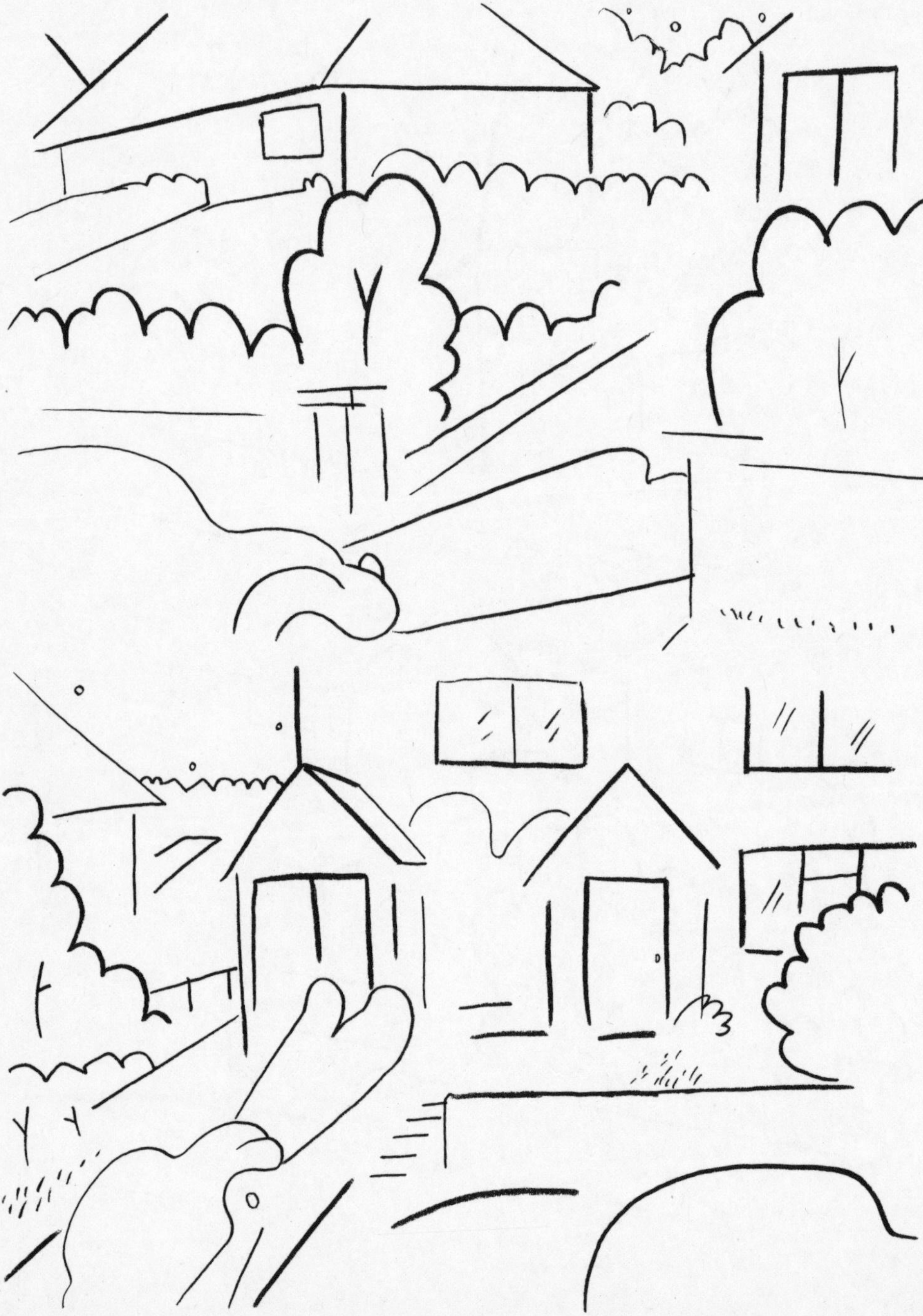

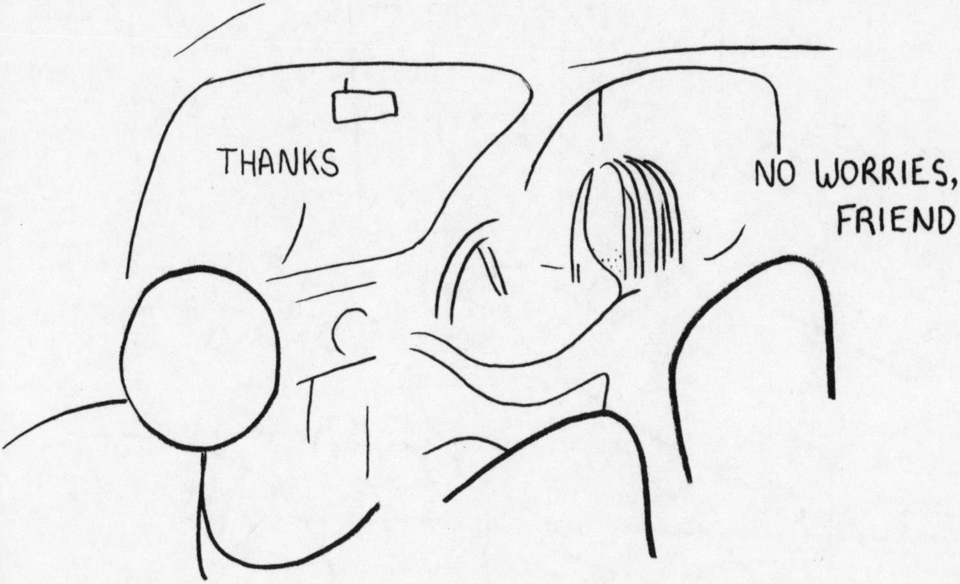
THANKS
NO WORRIES, FRIEND

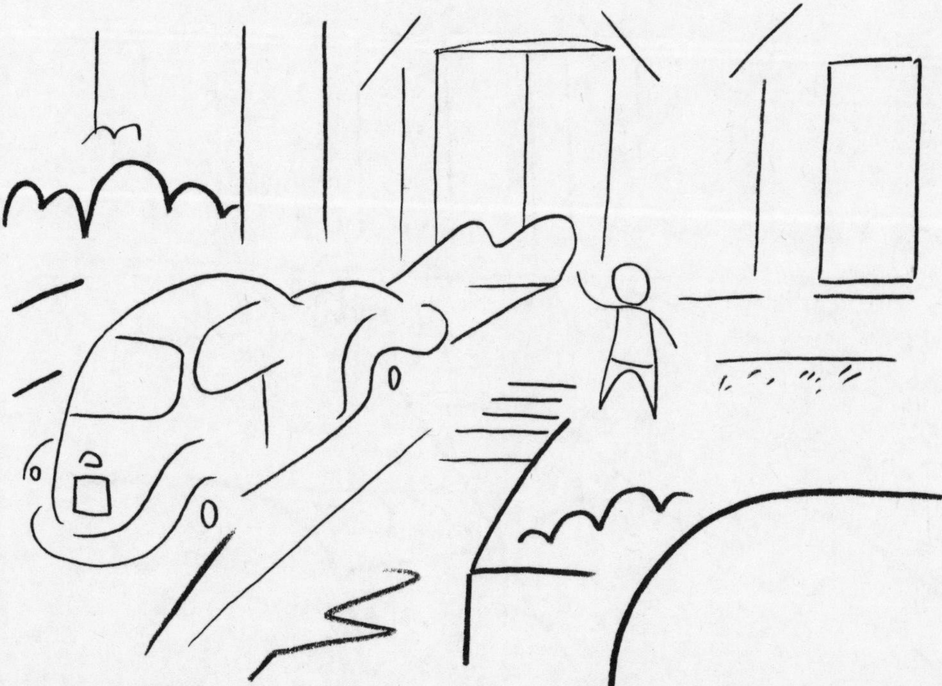

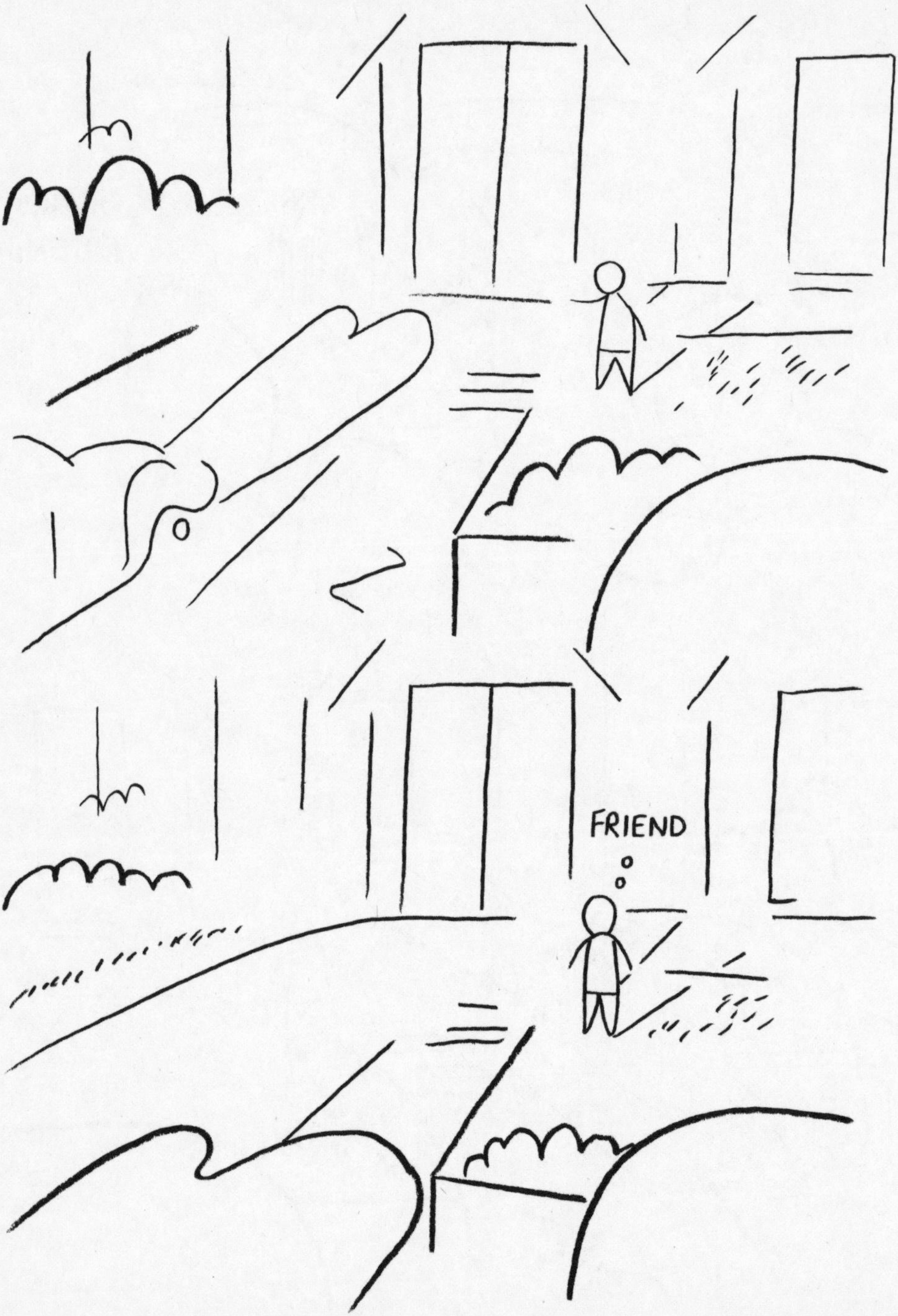
FRIEND

OR THE TIME OLI AND I WENT
SWIMMING IN THE THAMES

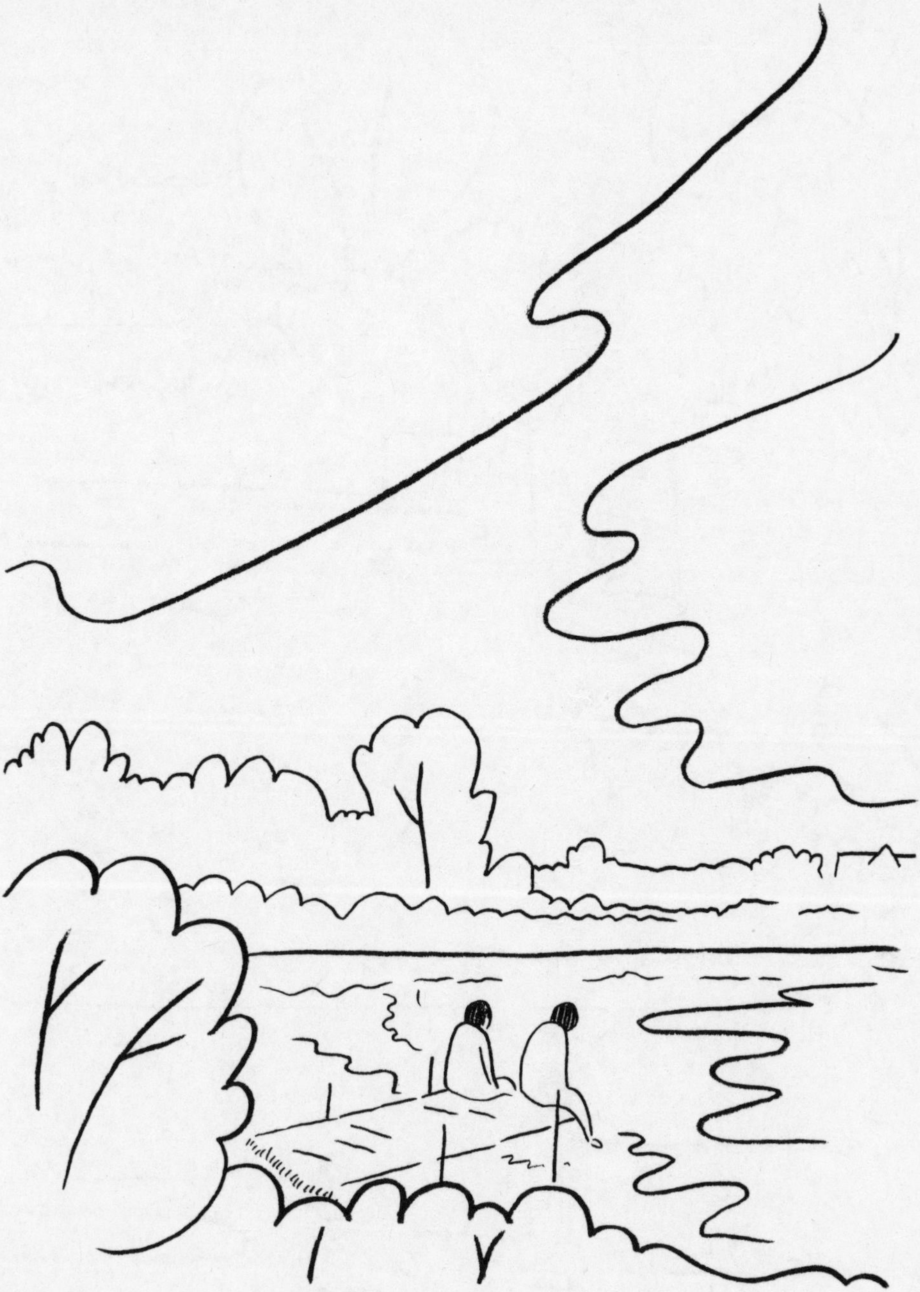

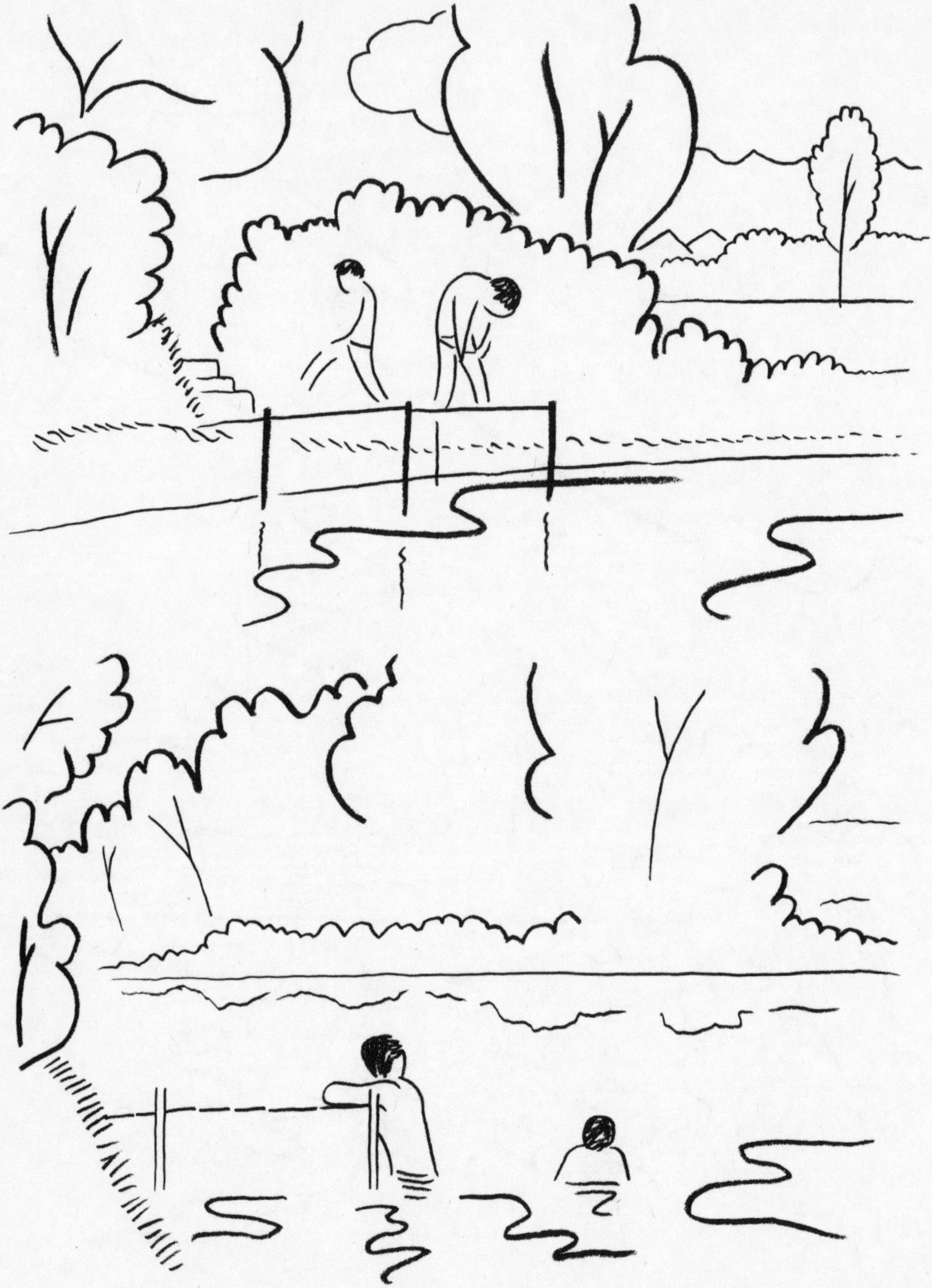

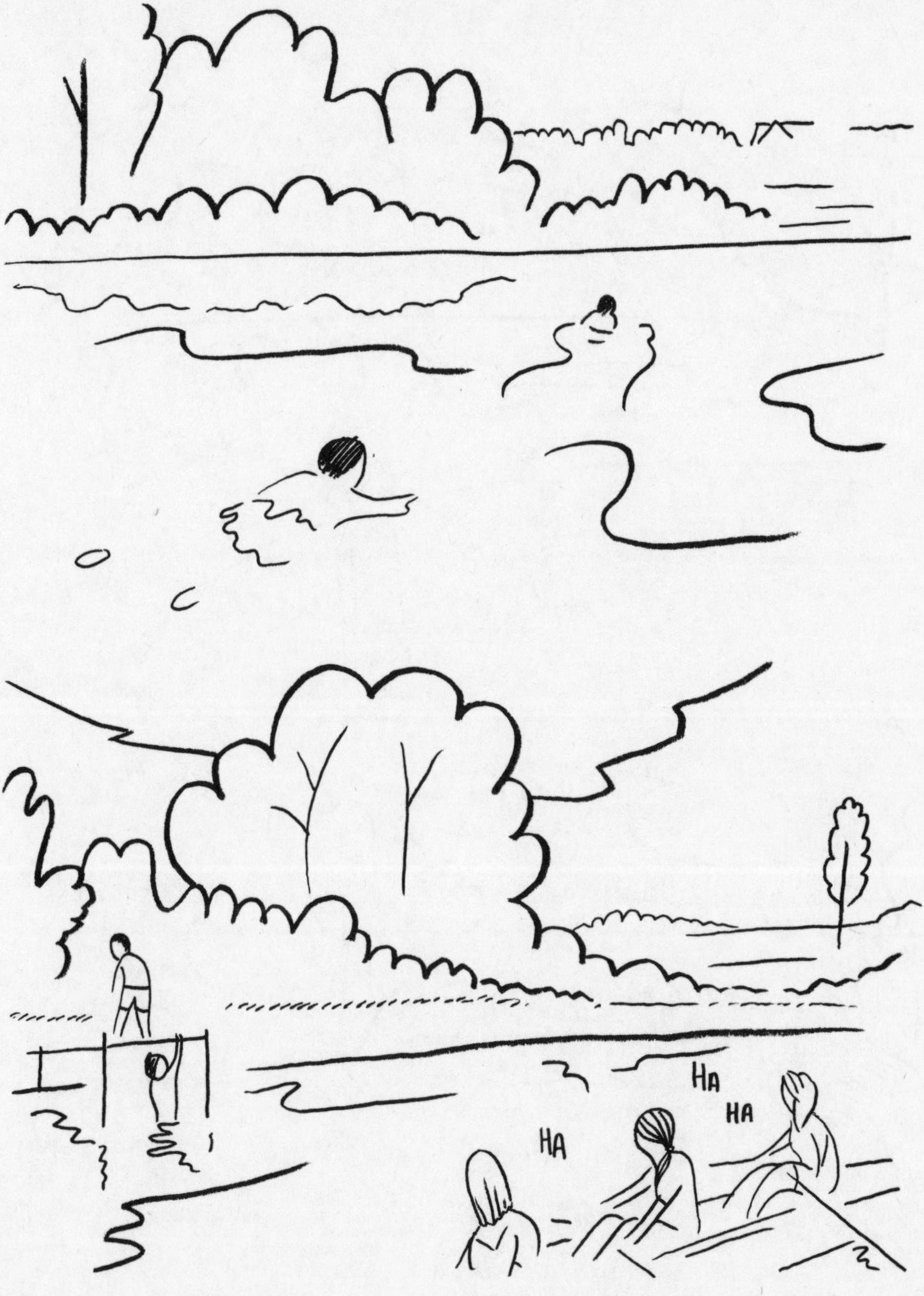
HA
HA
HA

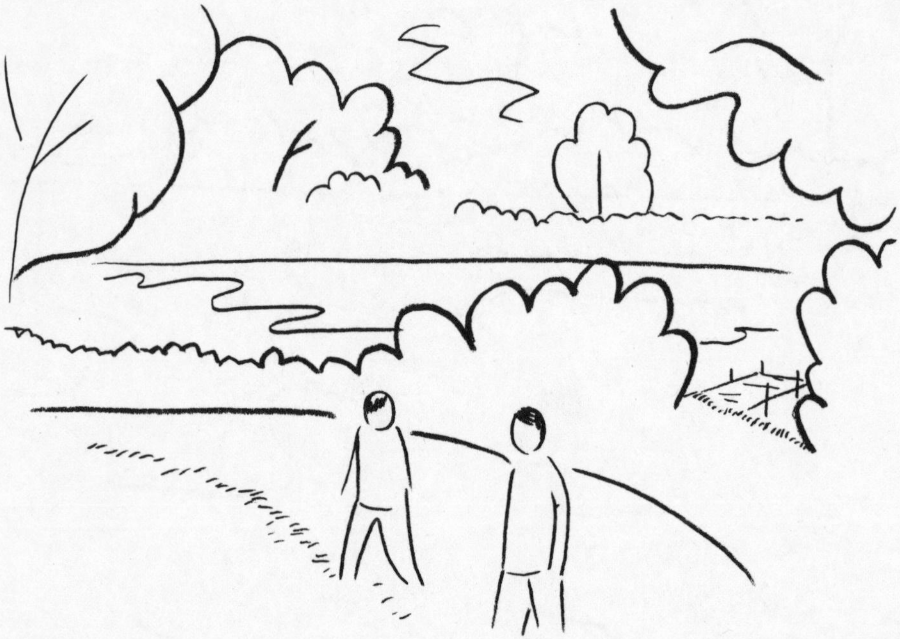

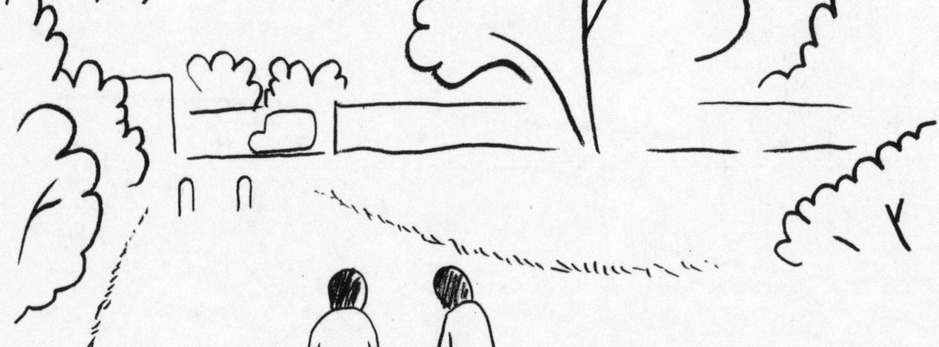

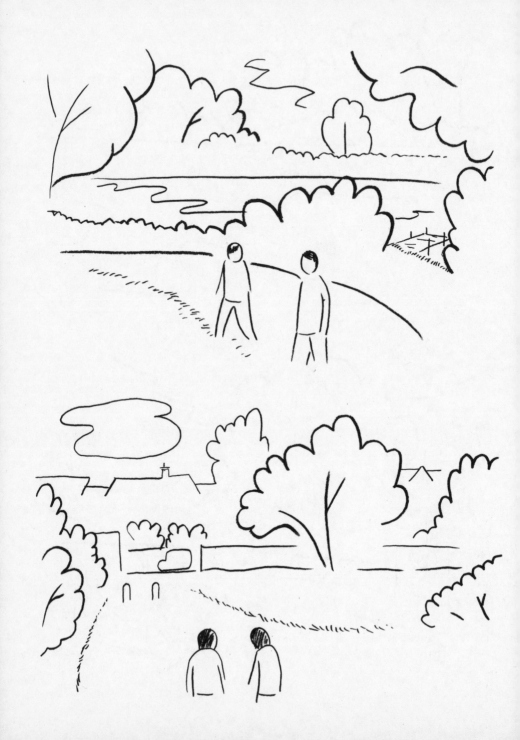

AT SOME PARTY

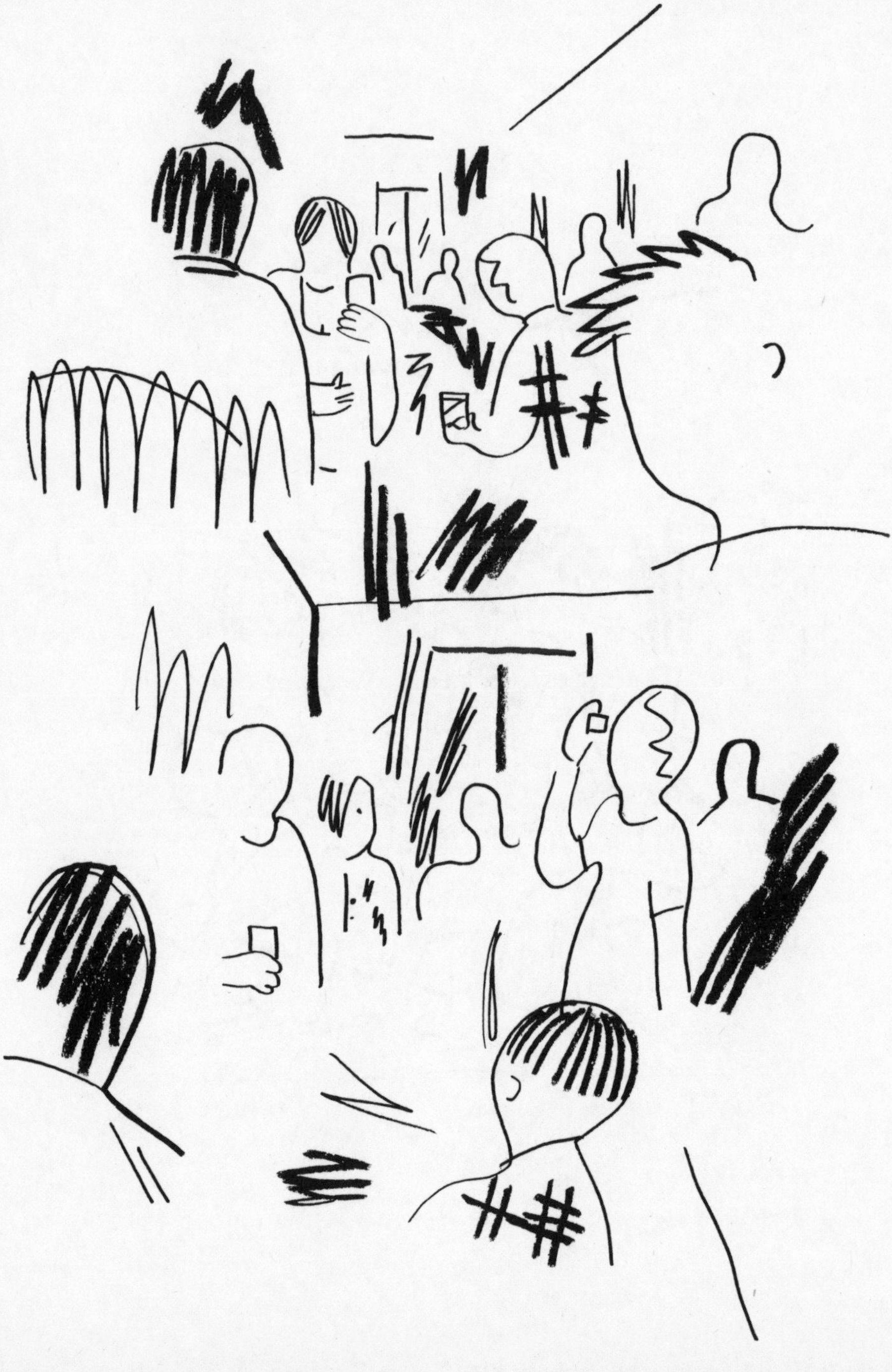

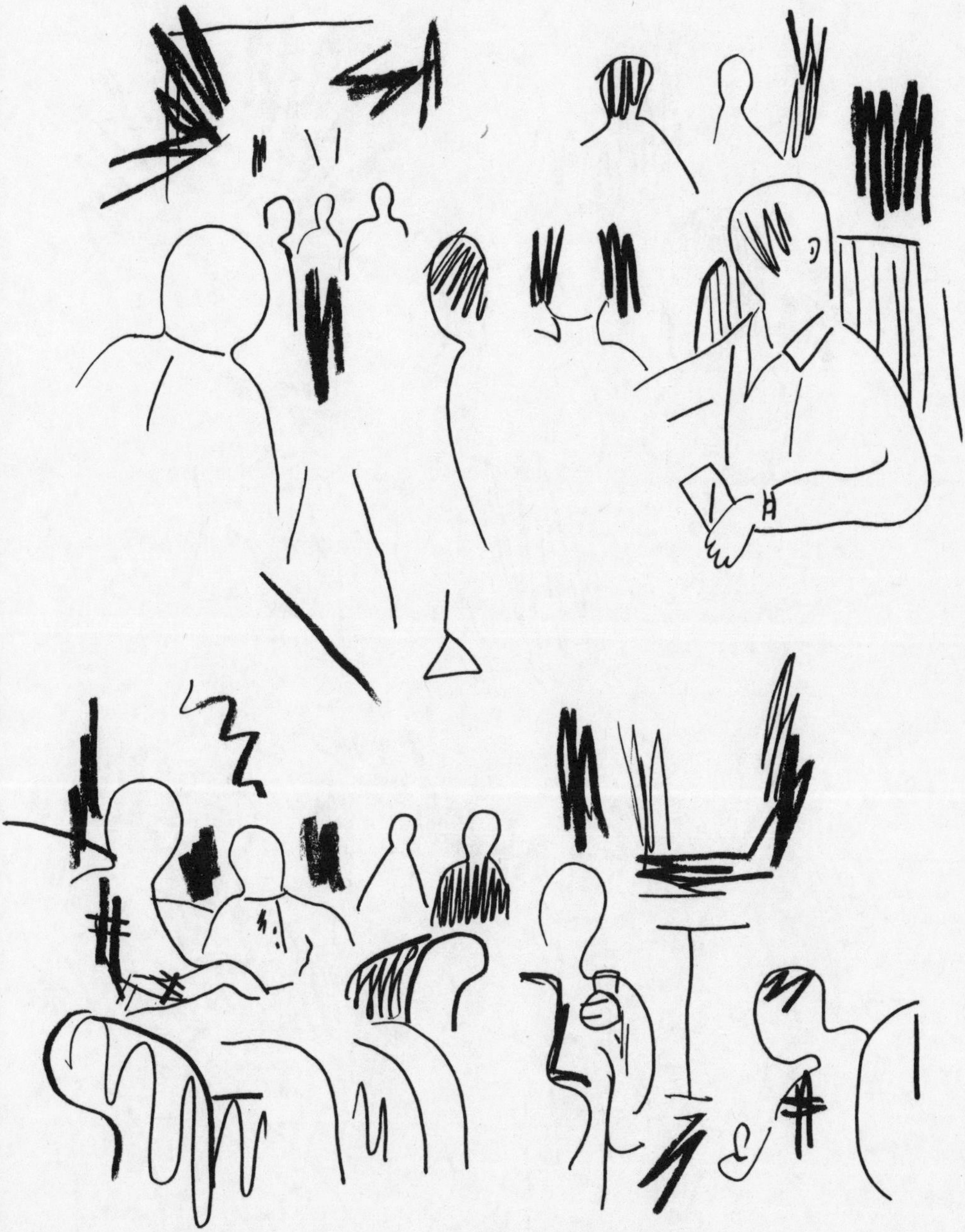

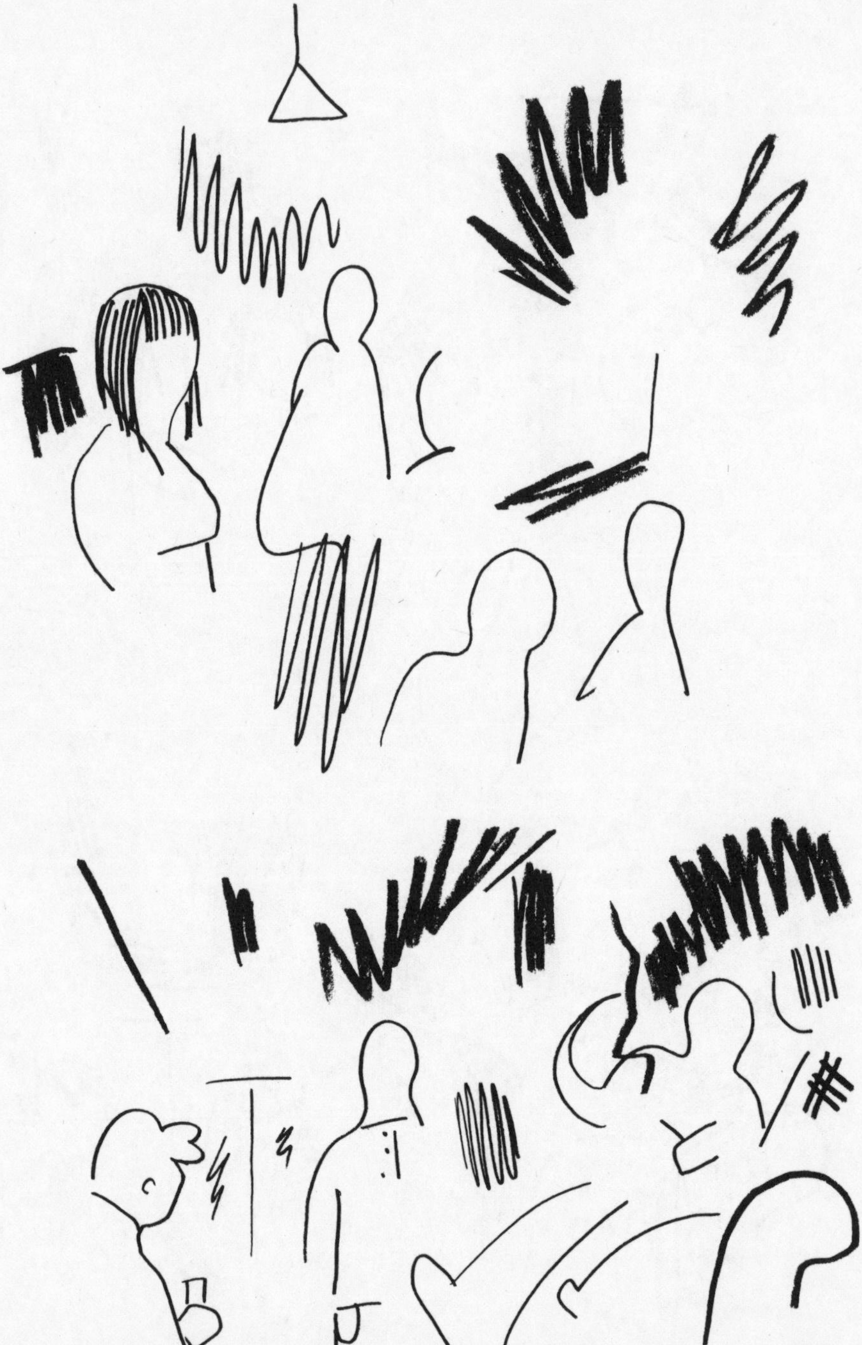

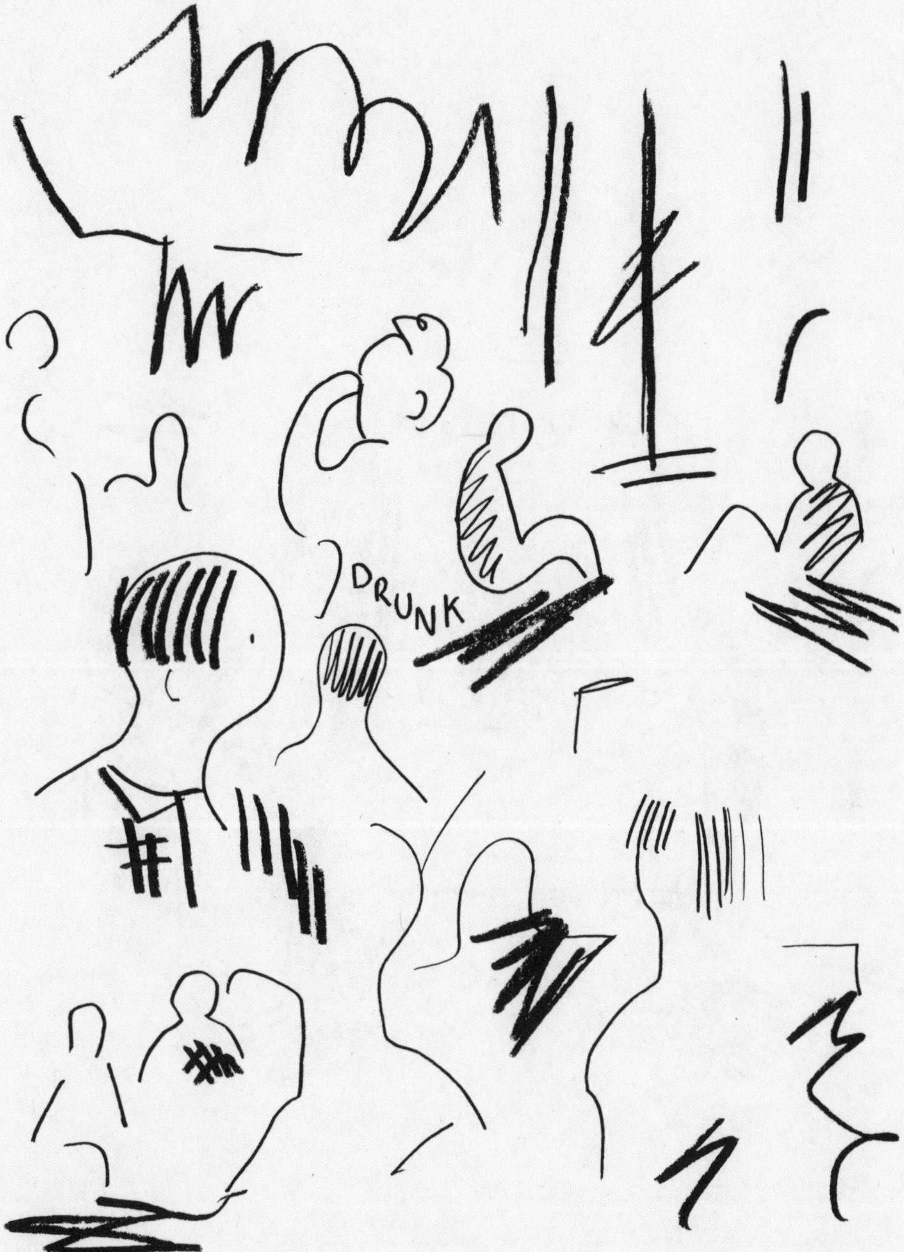
DRUNK

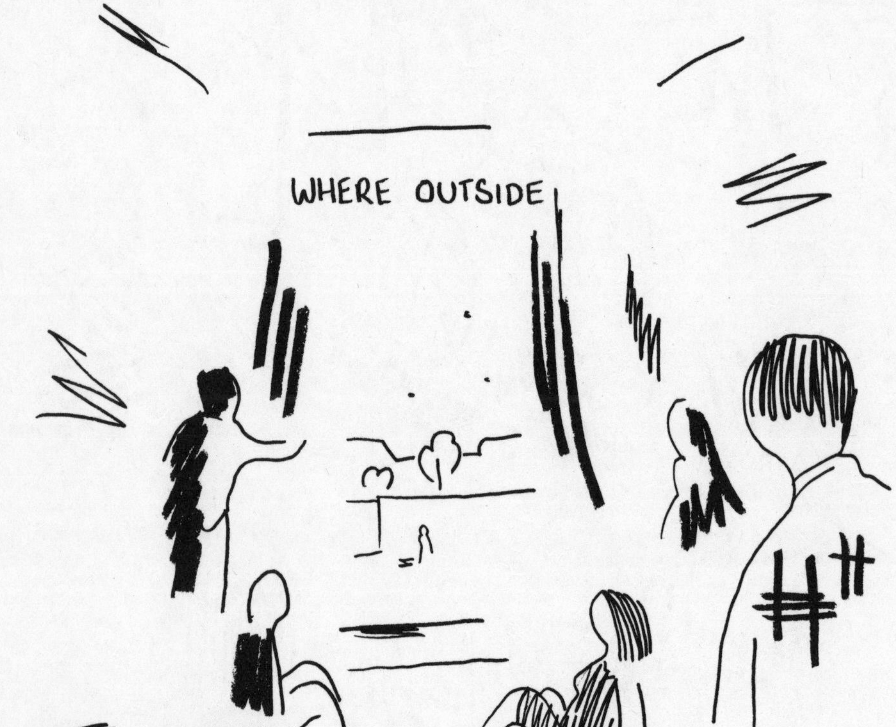
WHERE OUTSIDE

TOM WAS TRYING

AND FAILING

TO ESCAPE

THE THING IS, I WAS SAD

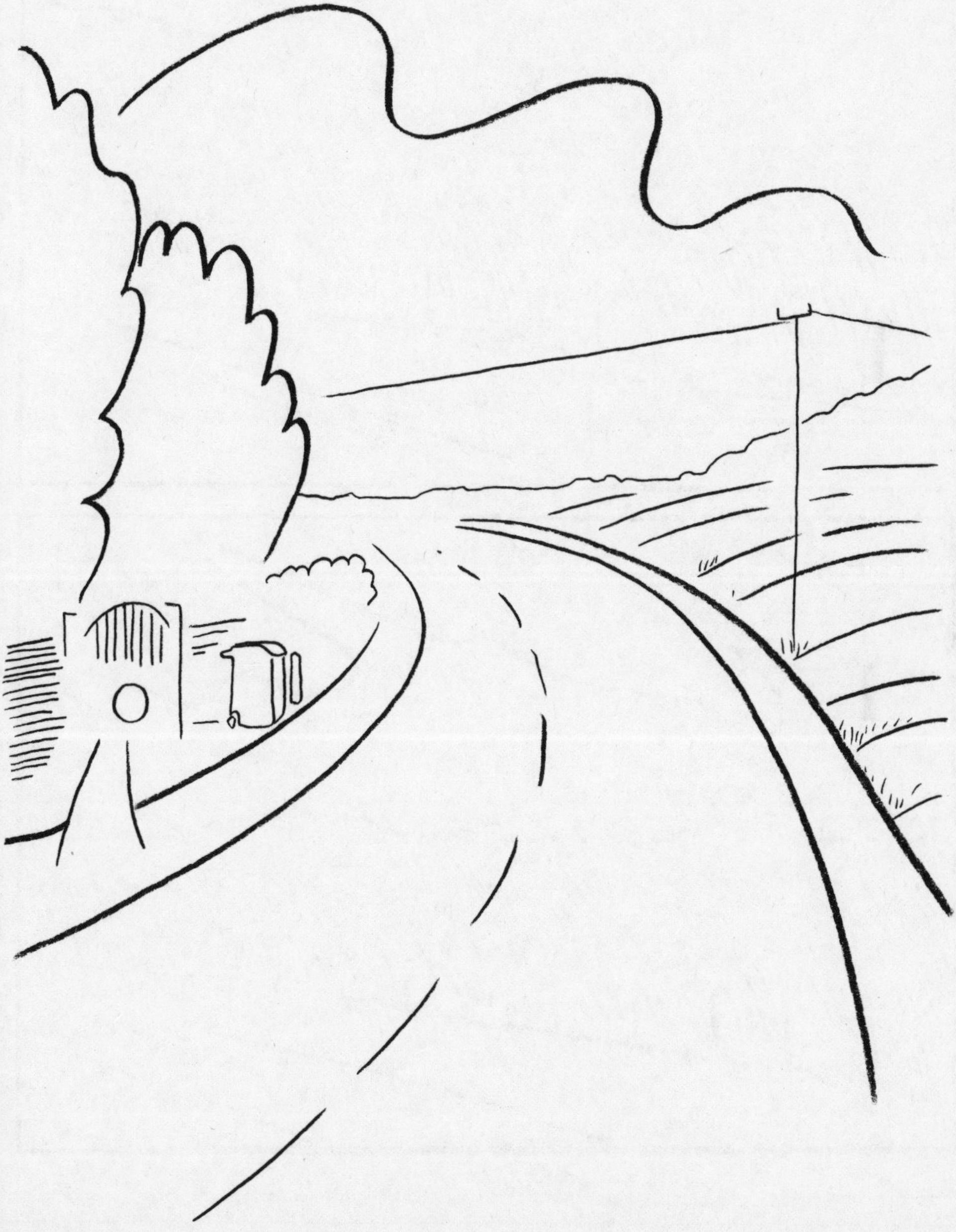

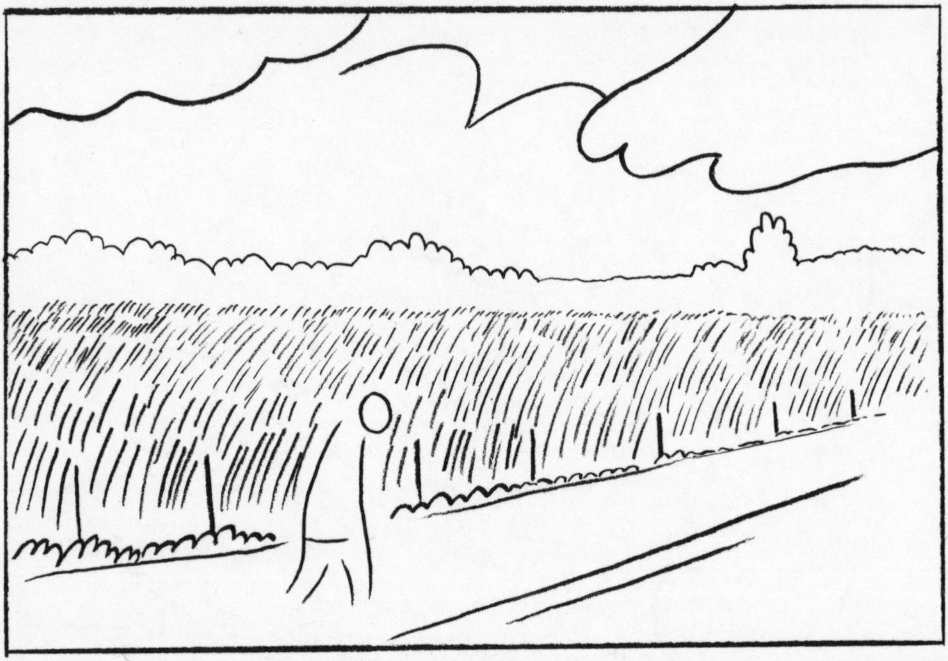
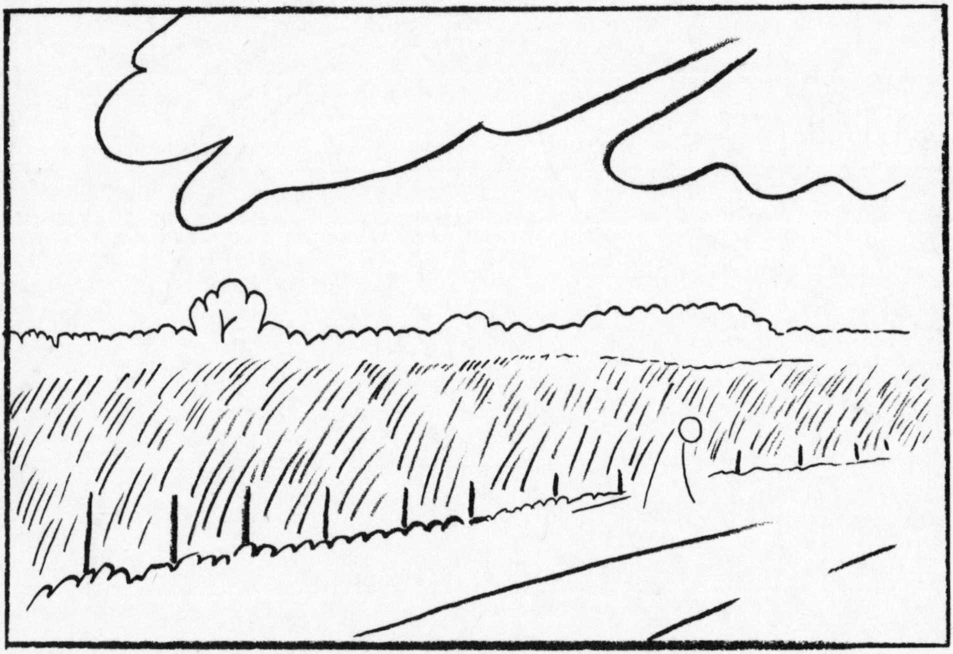

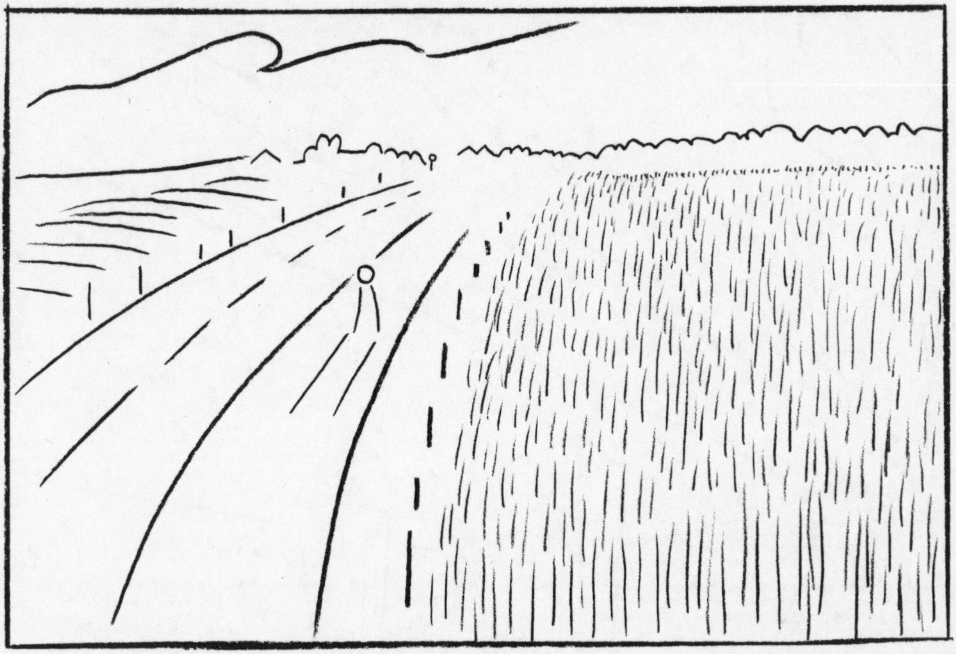

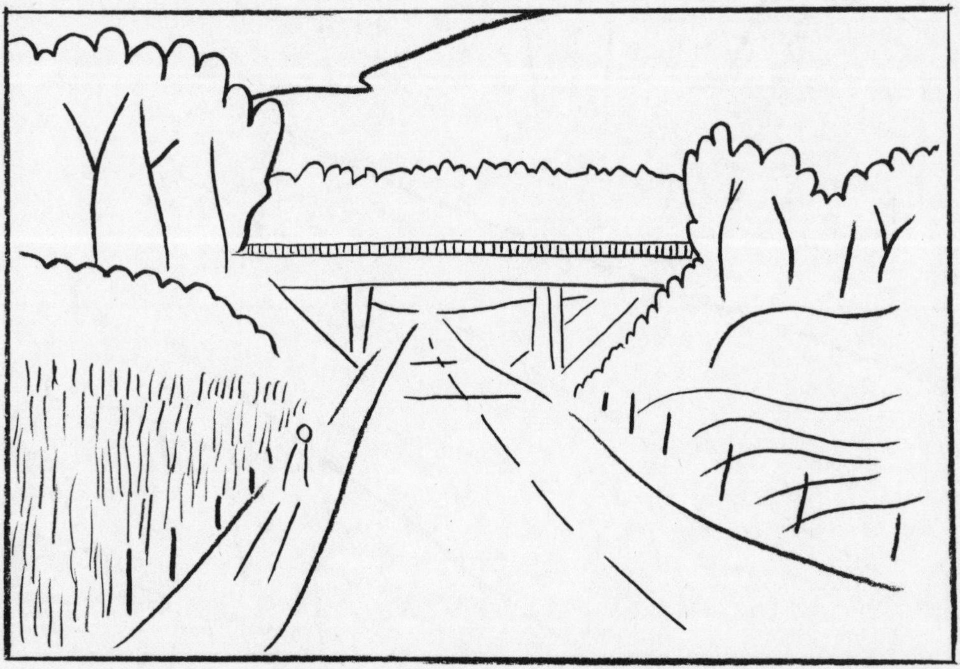

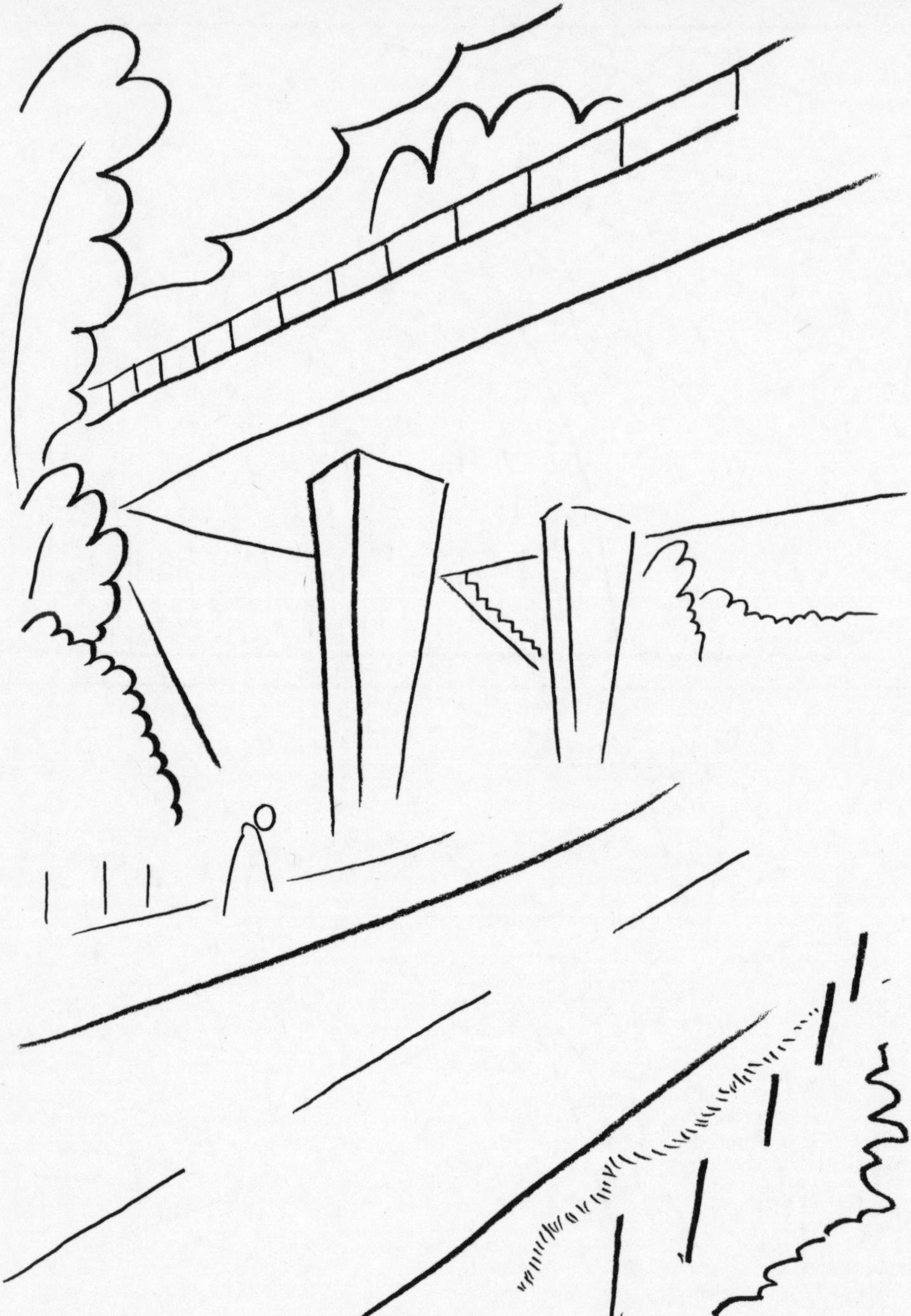

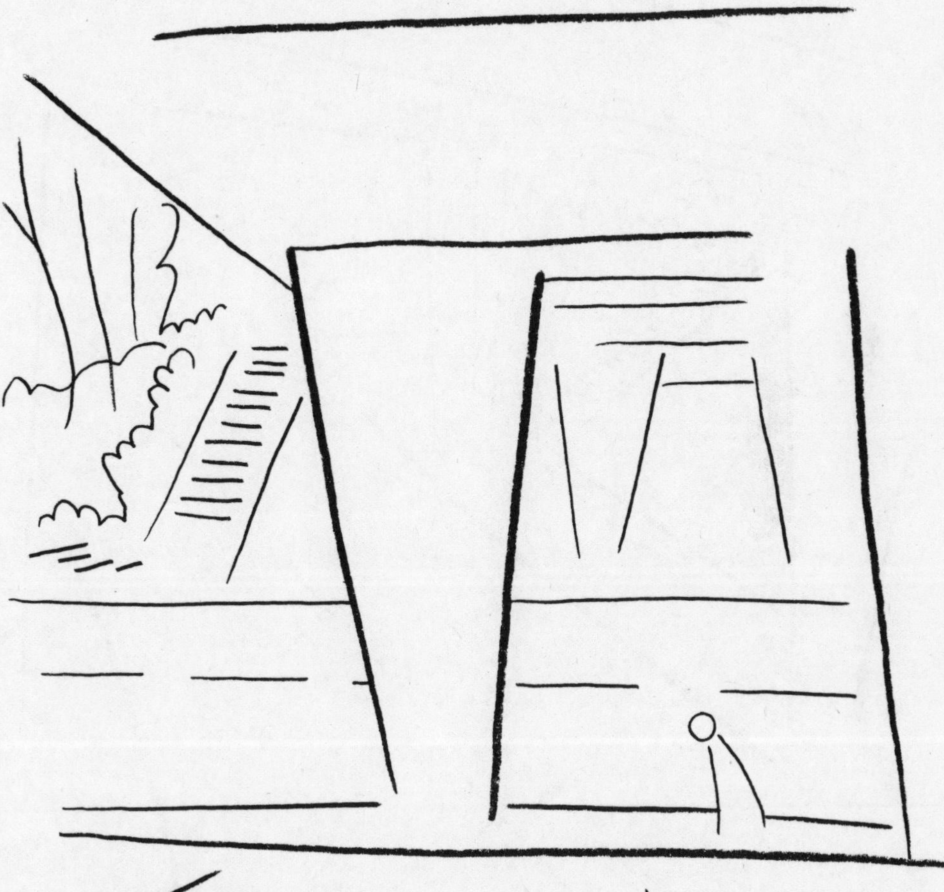

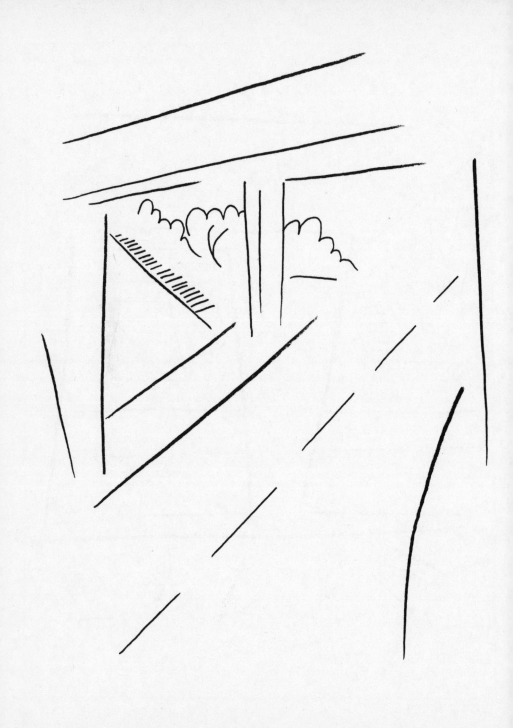

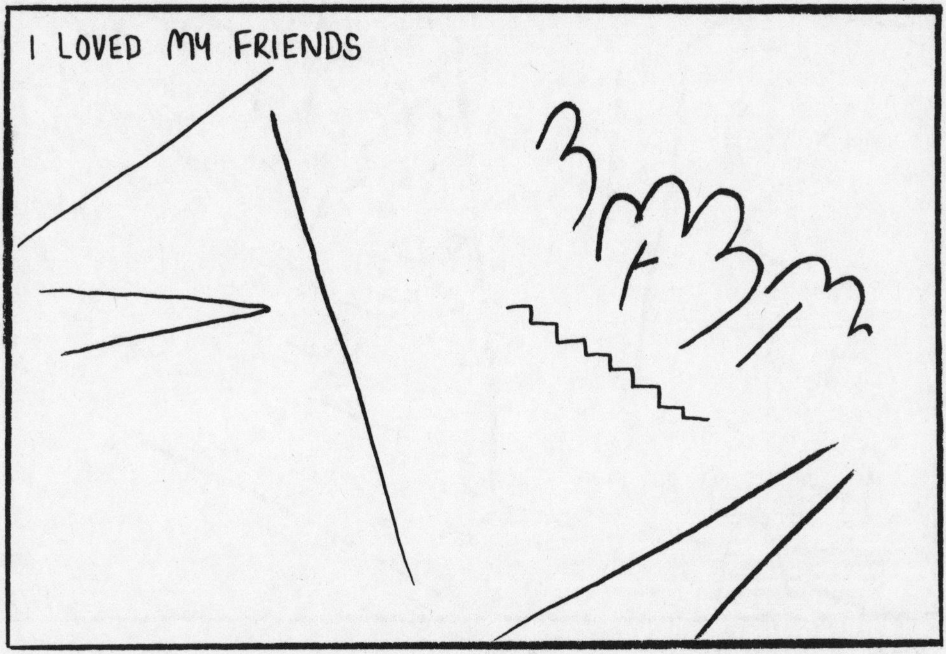
I LOVED MY FRIENDS

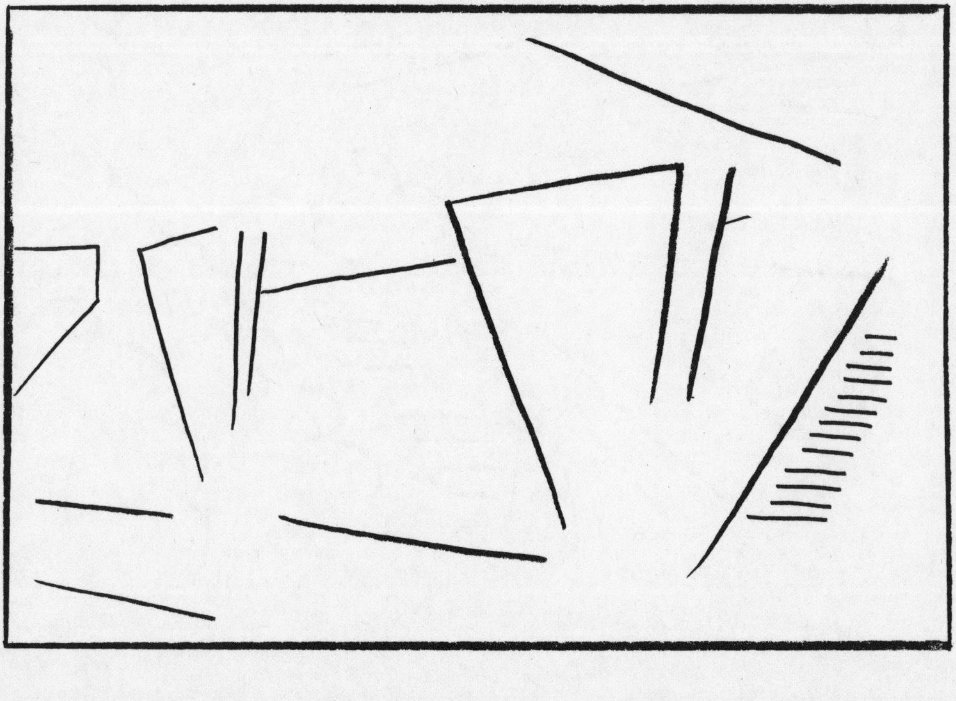

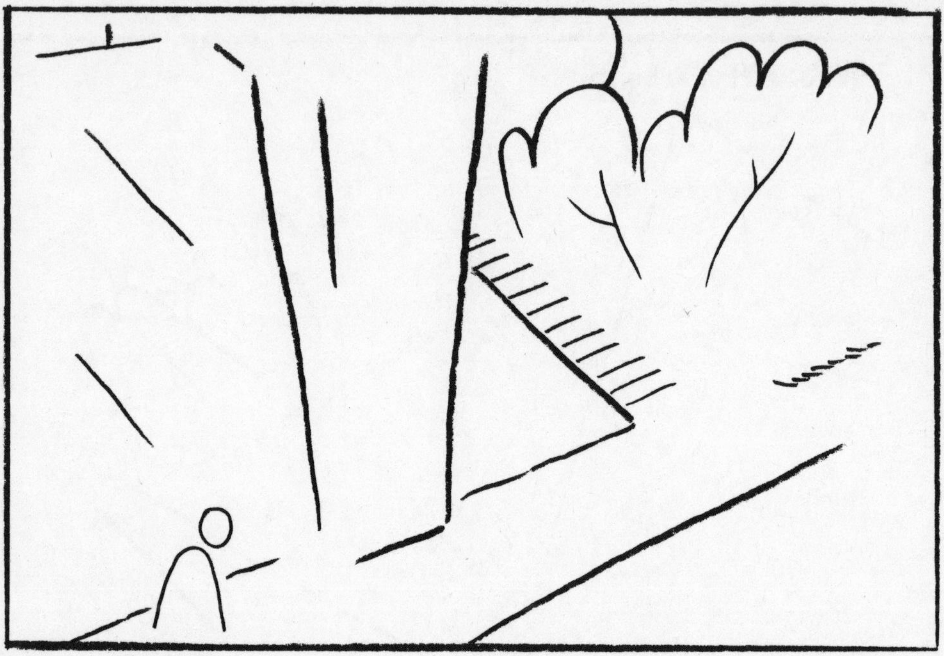

BUT I ACHED

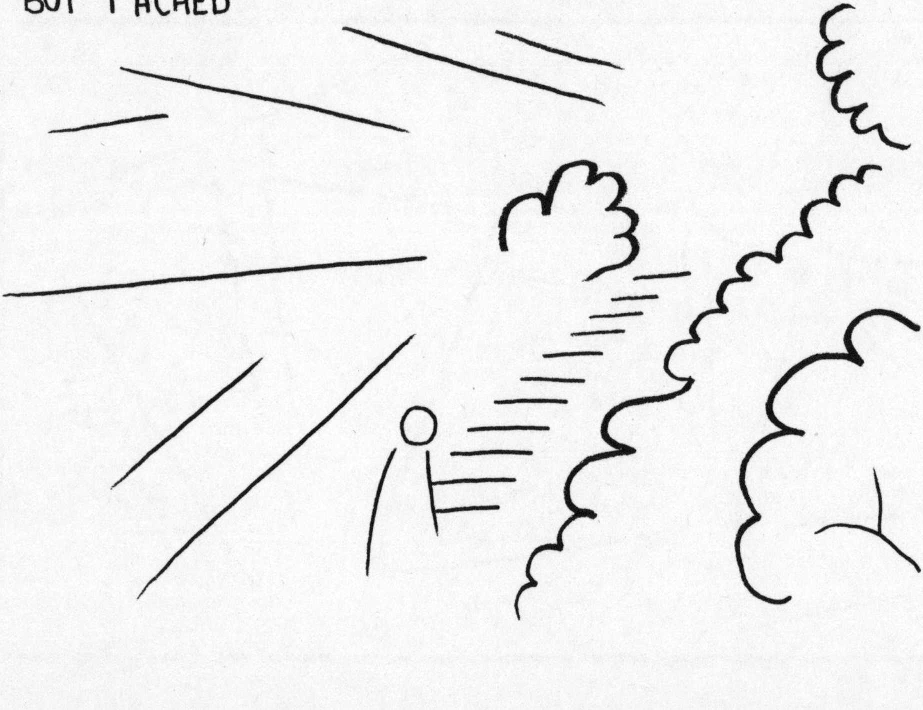

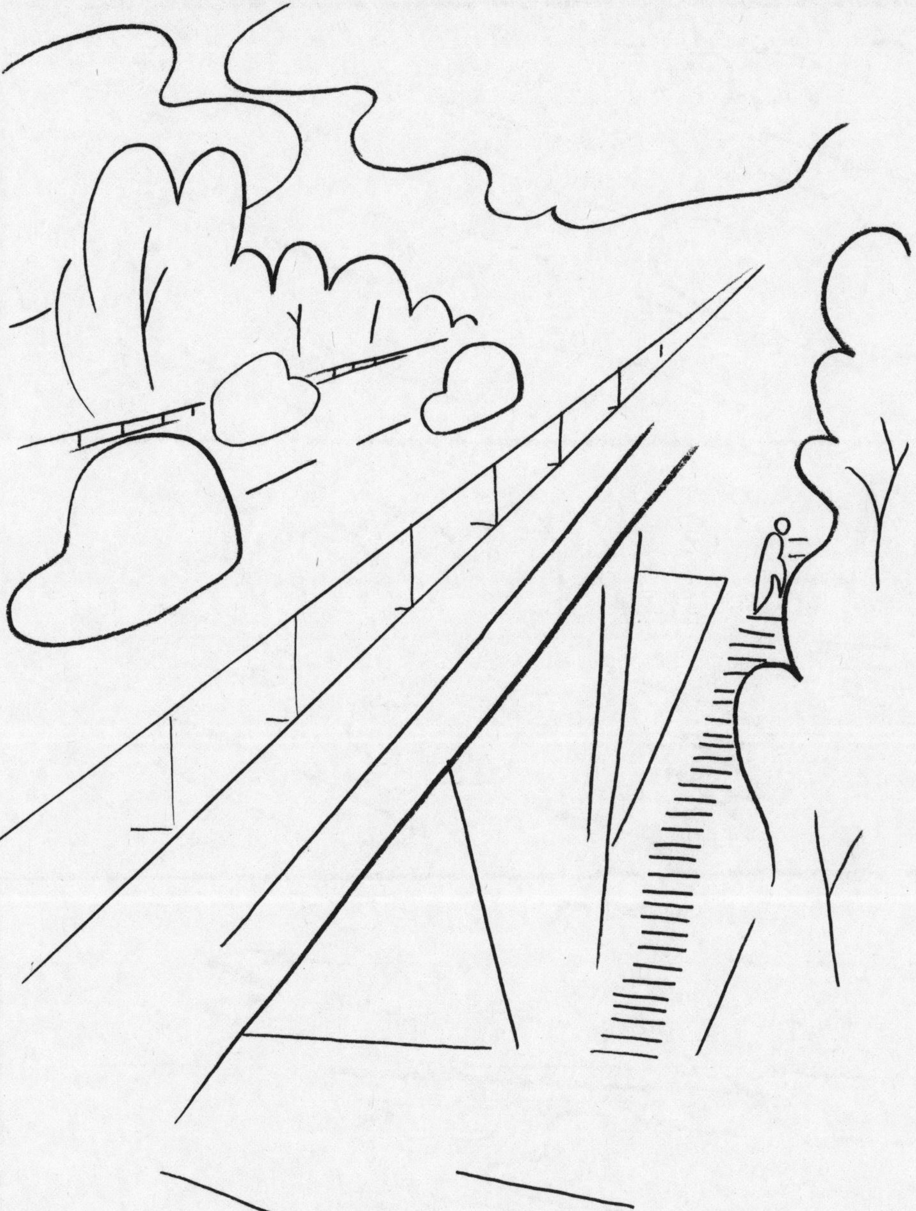

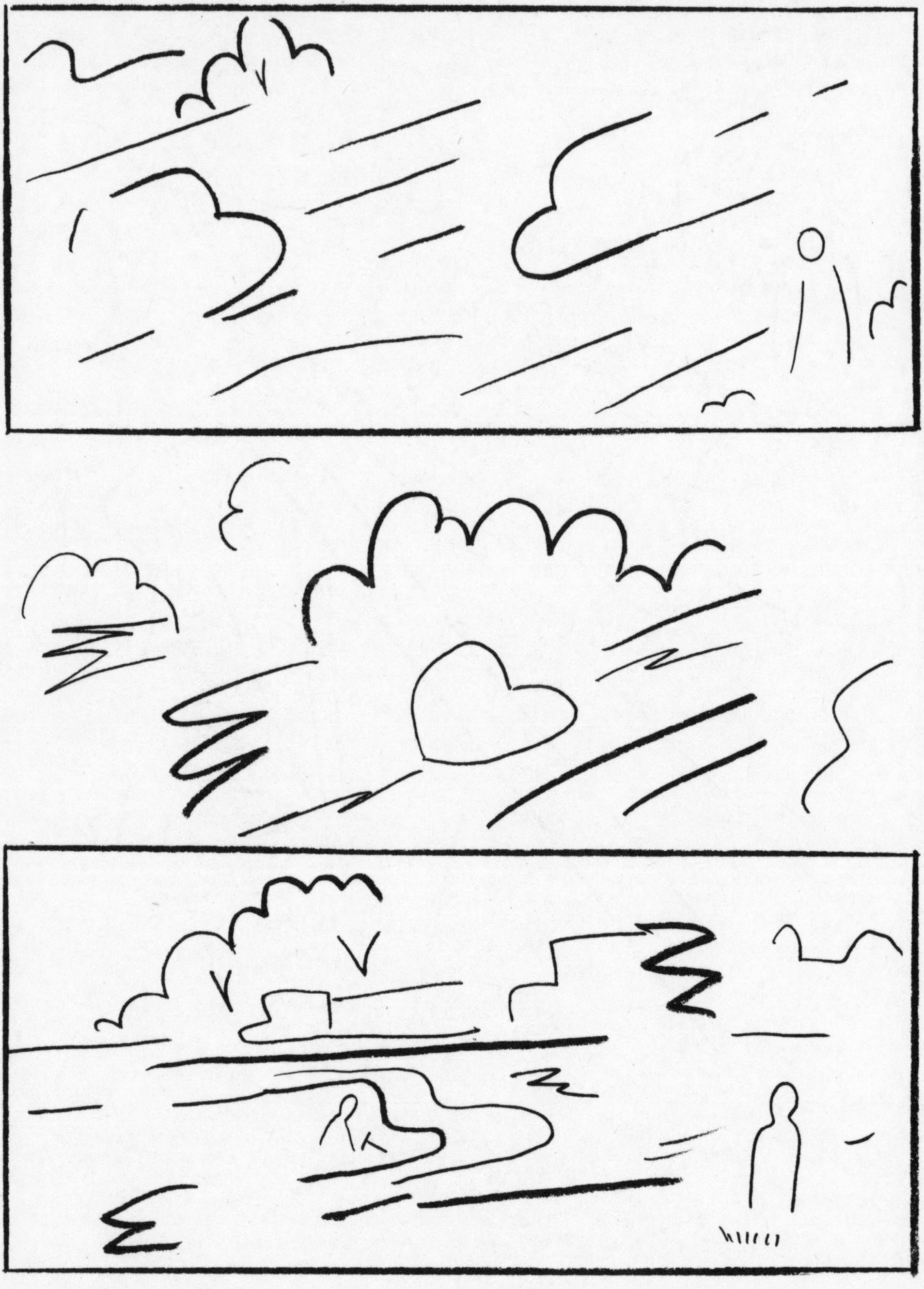

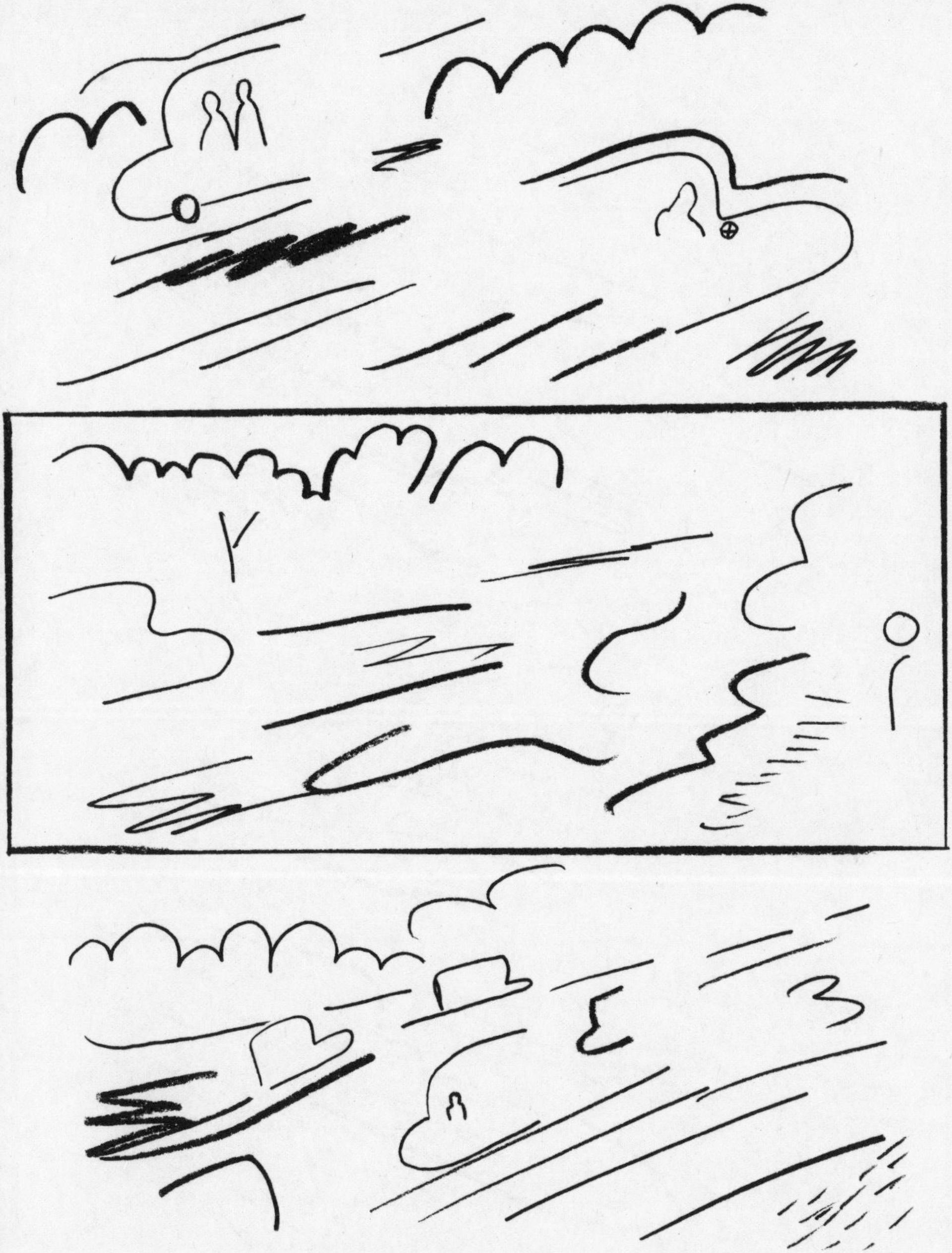

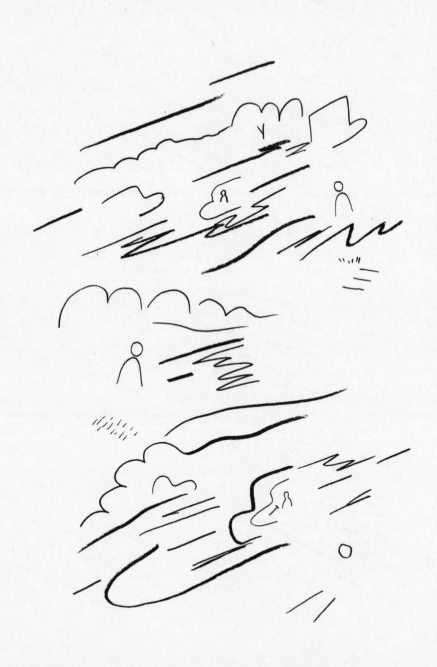

TO LEAVE

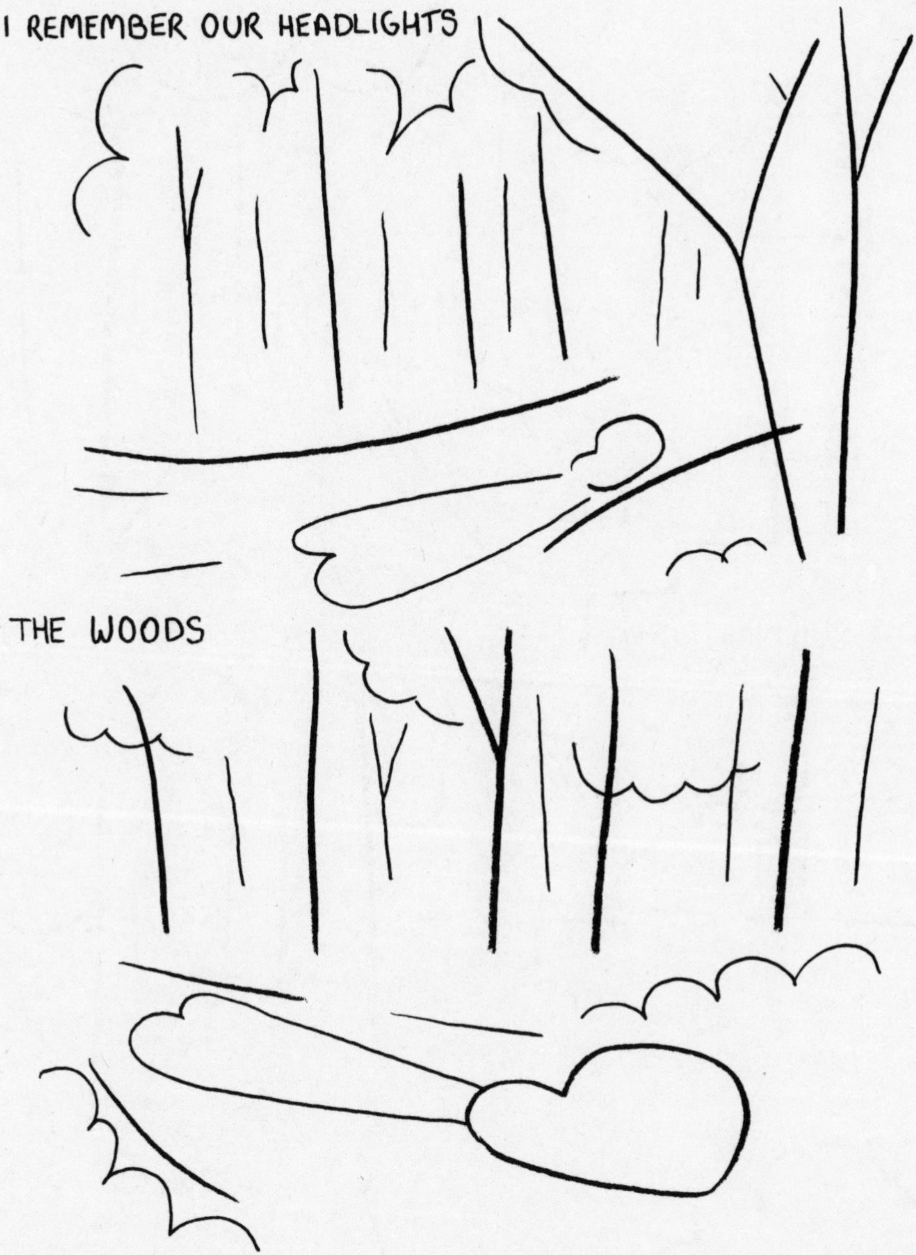
I REMEMBER OUR HEADLIGHTS
THE WOODS

PARKING

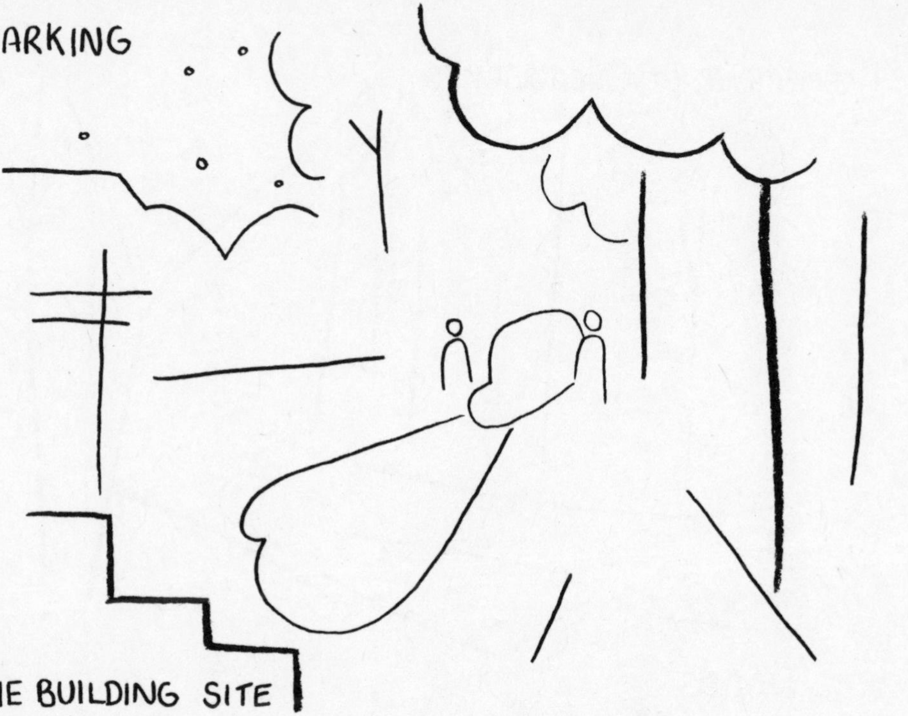

THE BUILDING SITE

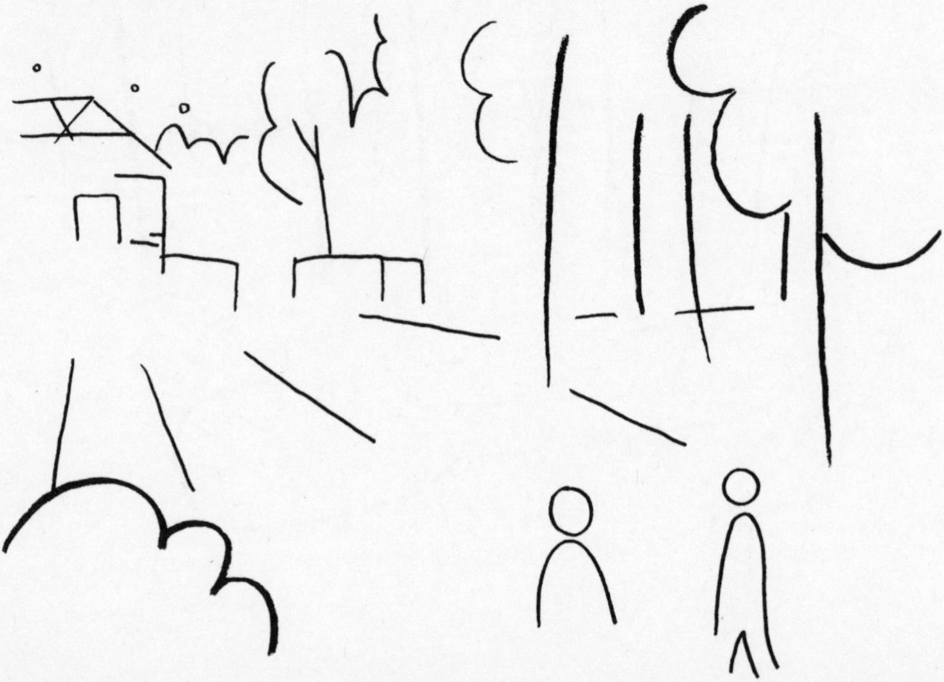

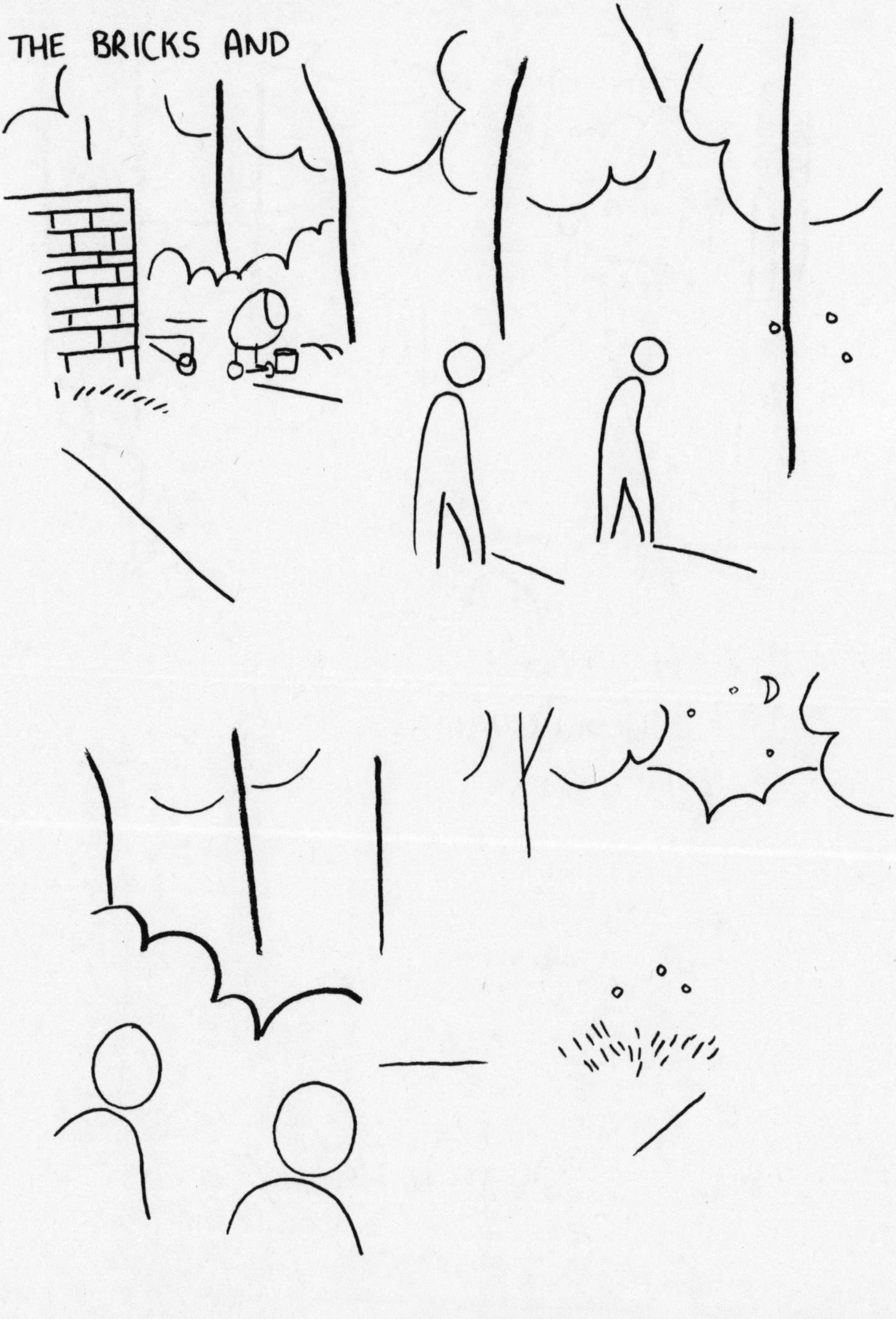
THE BRICKS AND

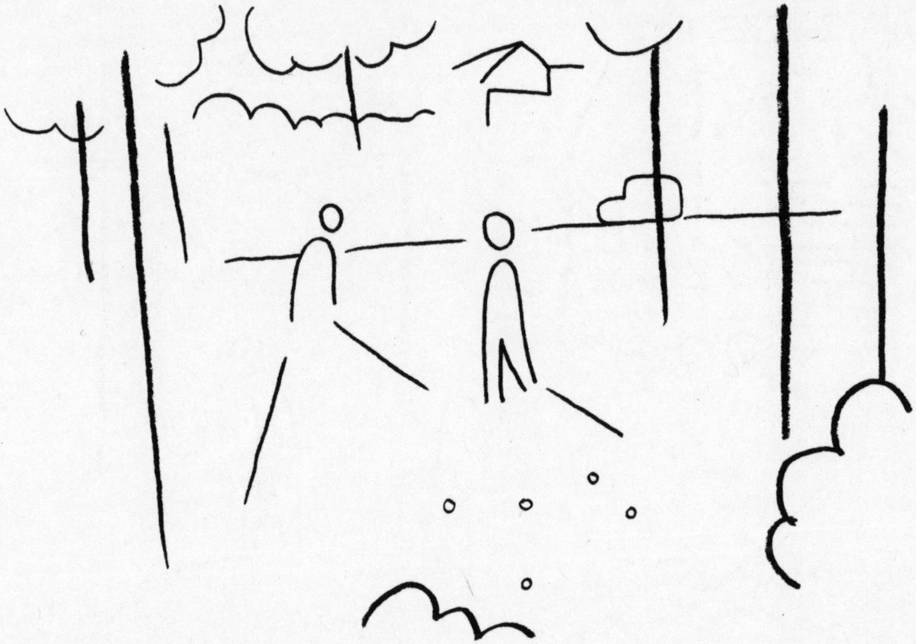

GLOW WORMS?

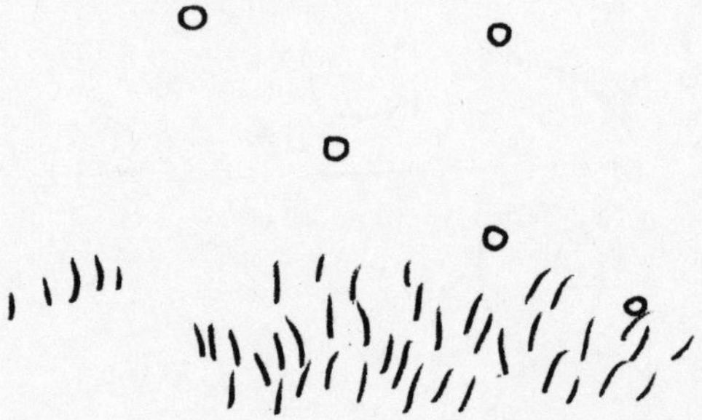

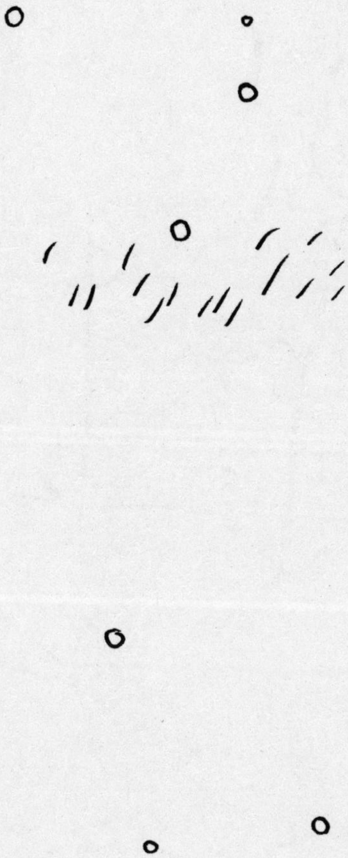

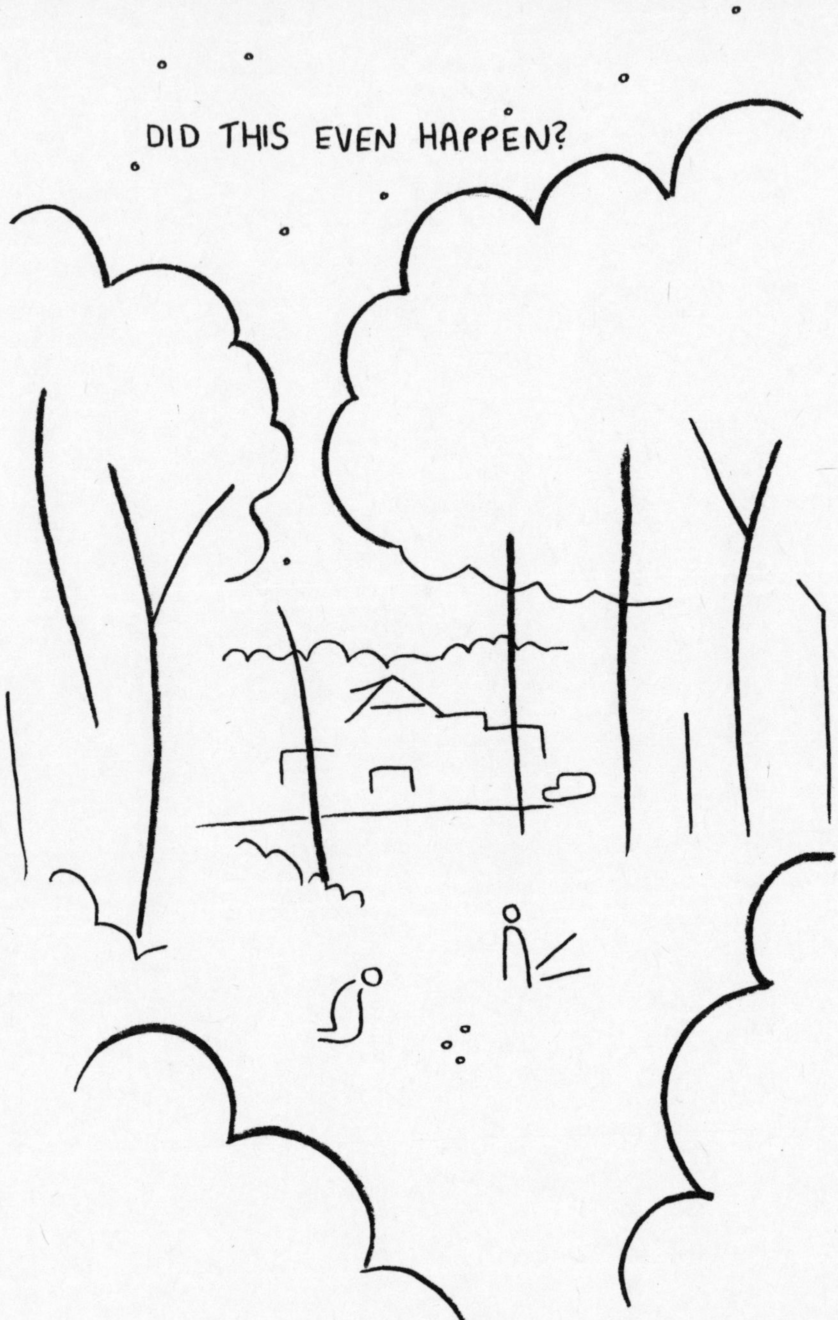
DID THIS EVEN HAPPEN?

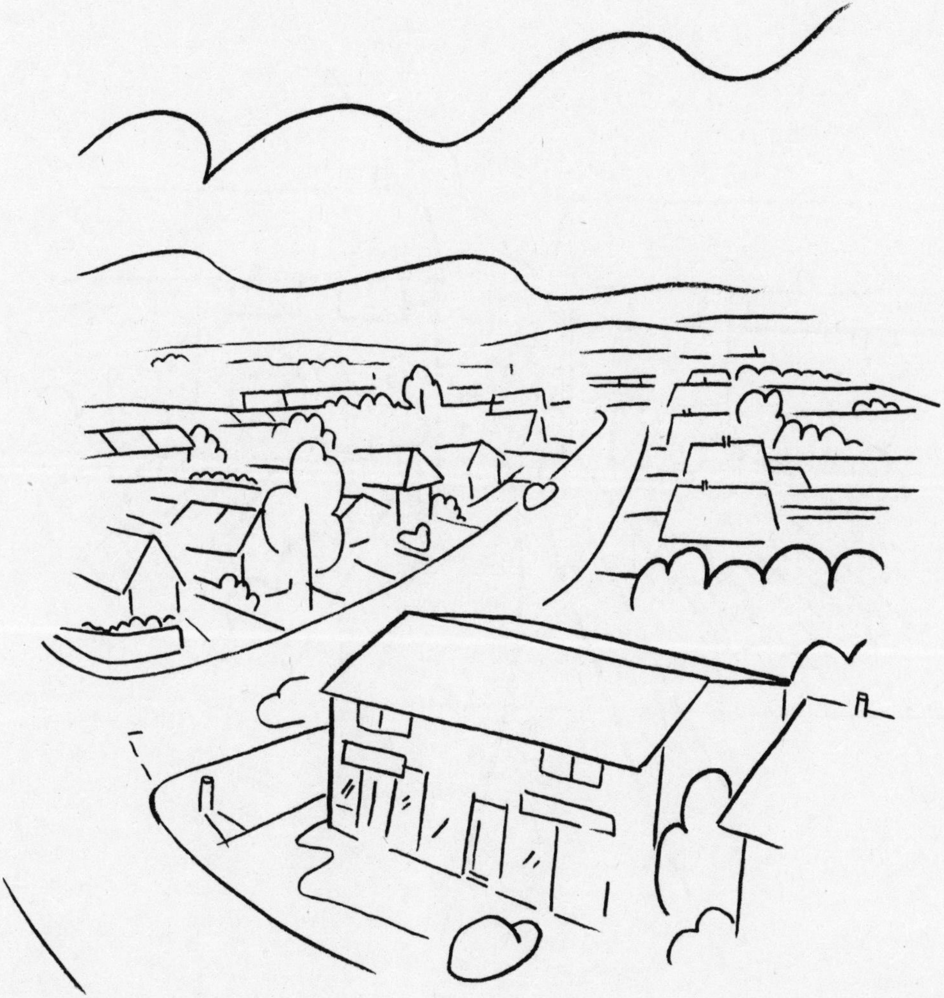

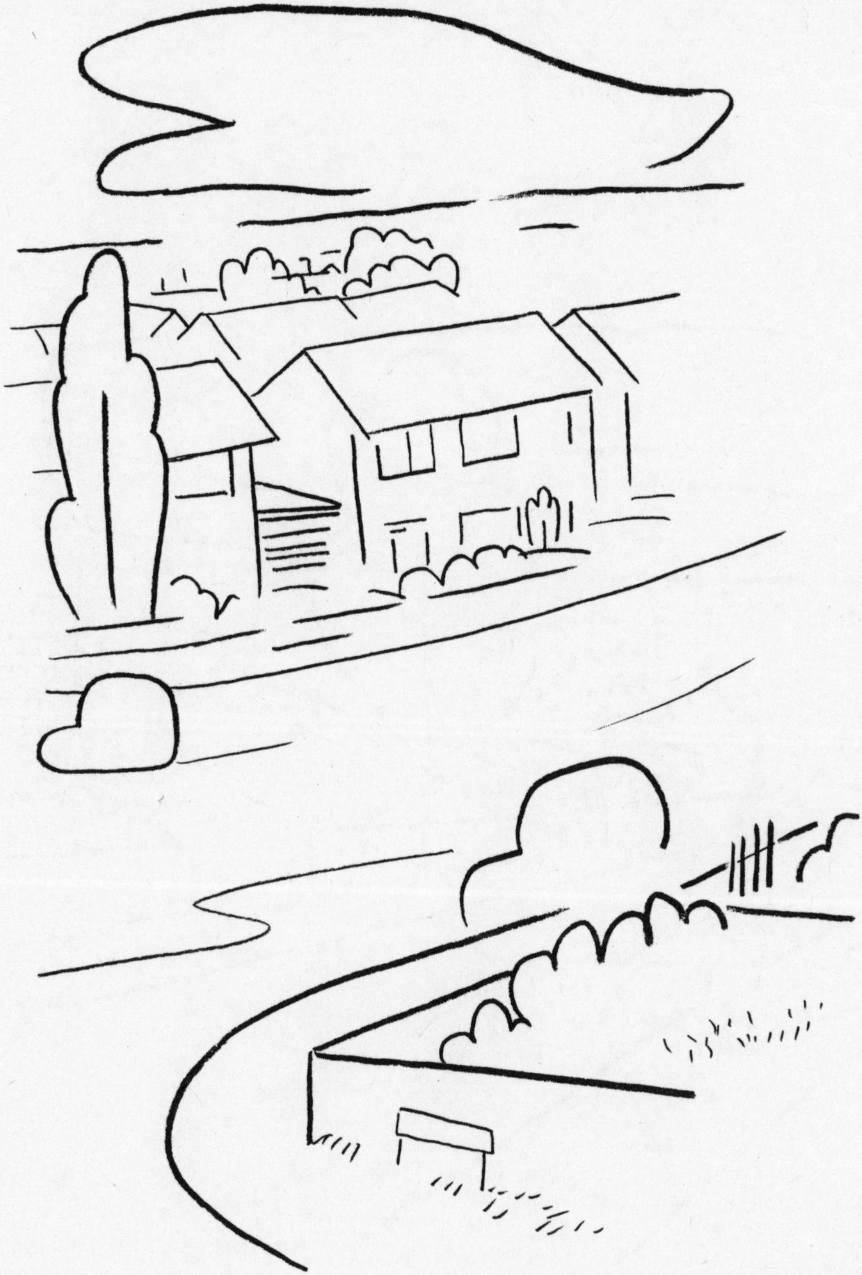

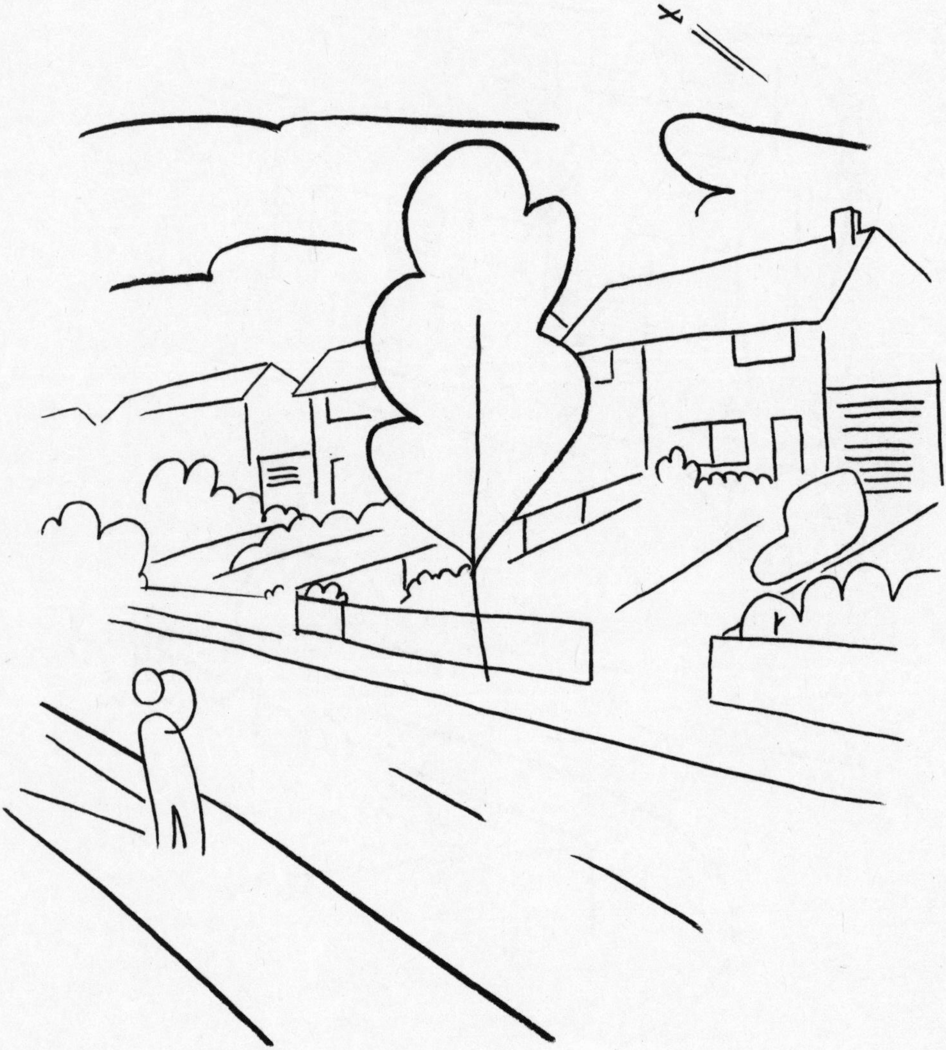

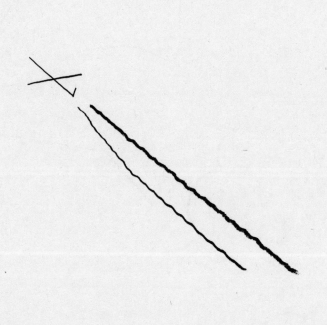

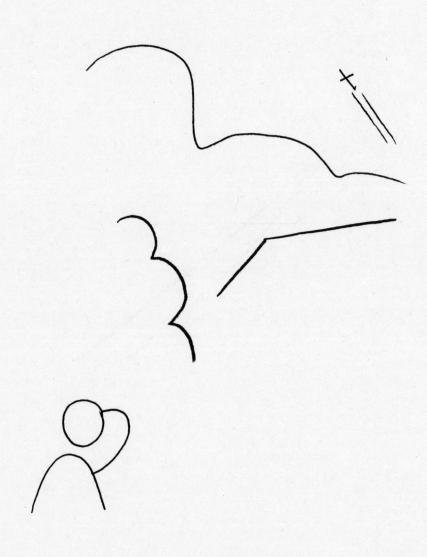

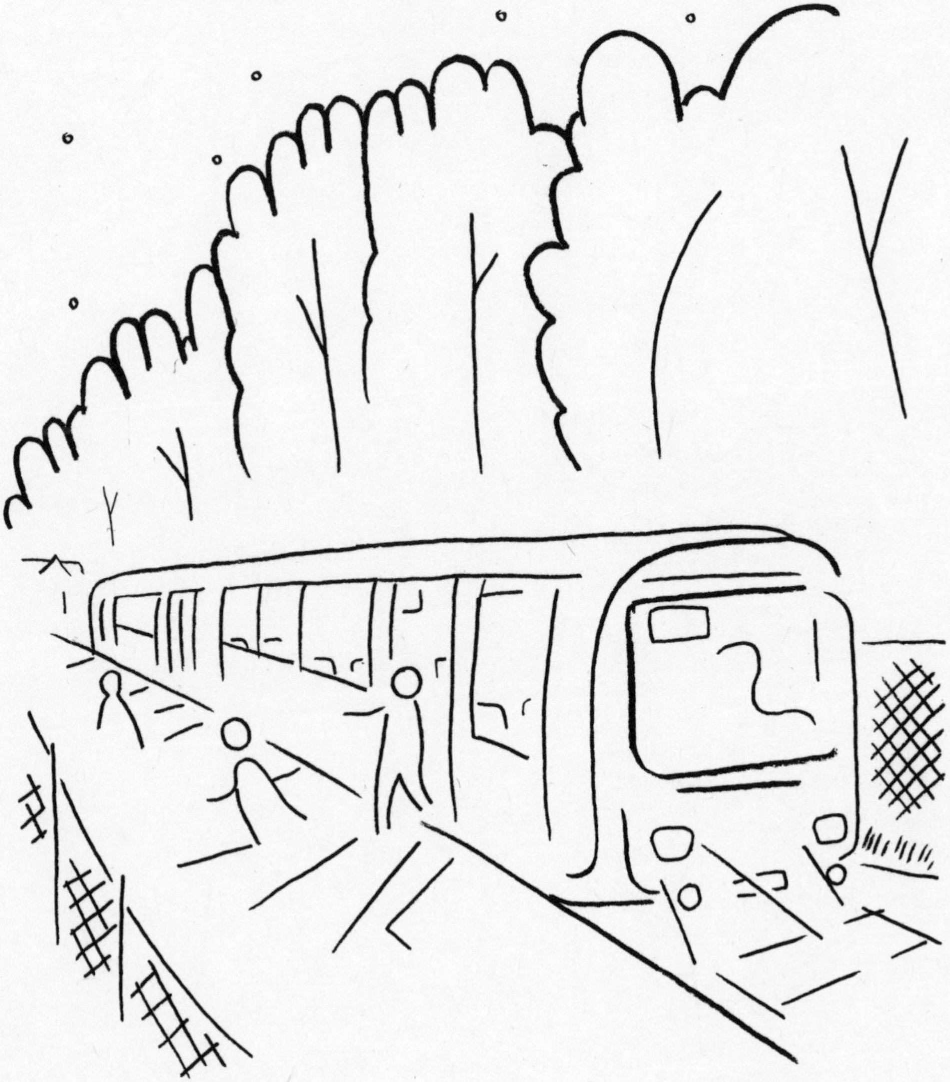

WHEN YOU ARE

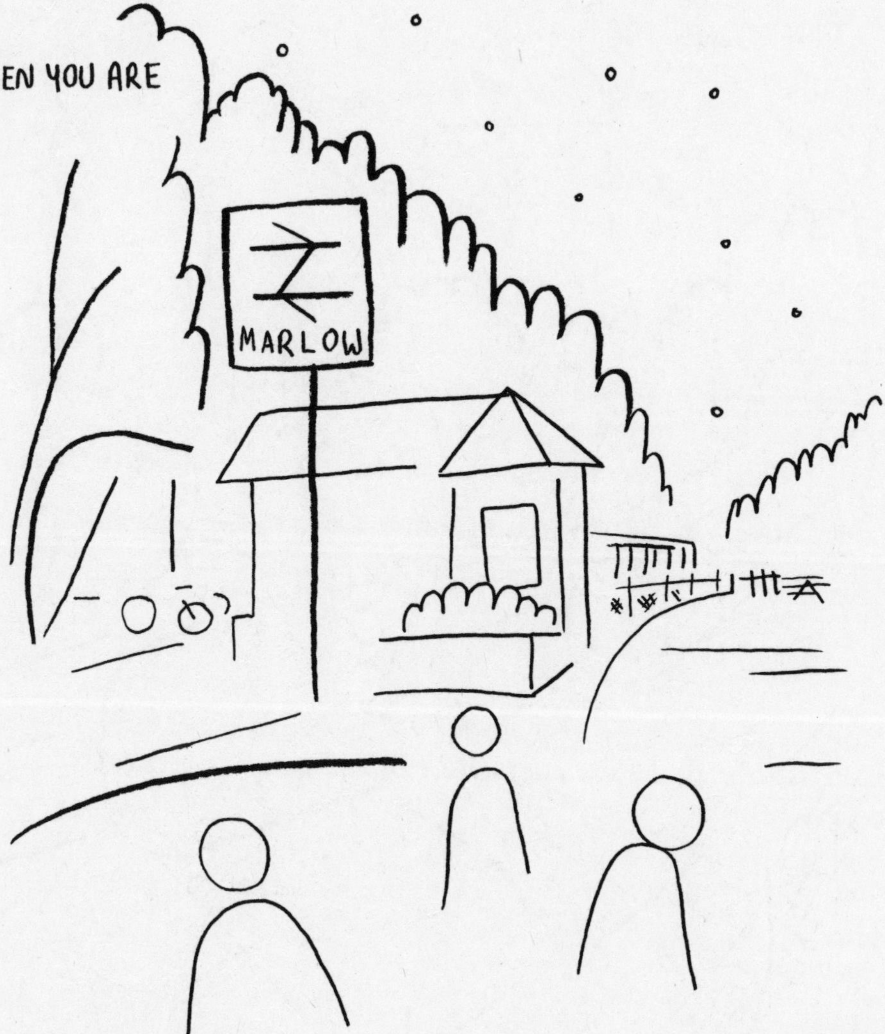
MARLOW

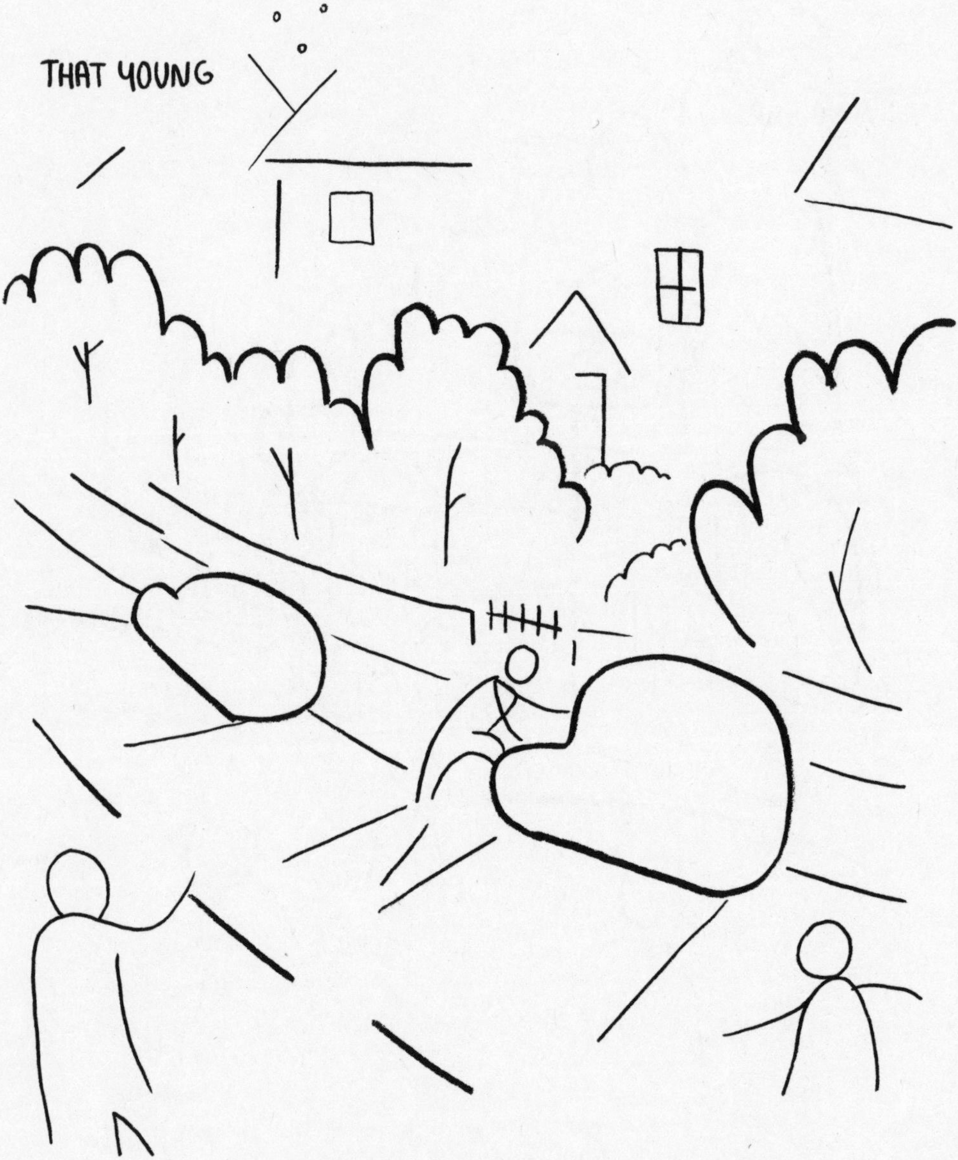
THAT YOUNG

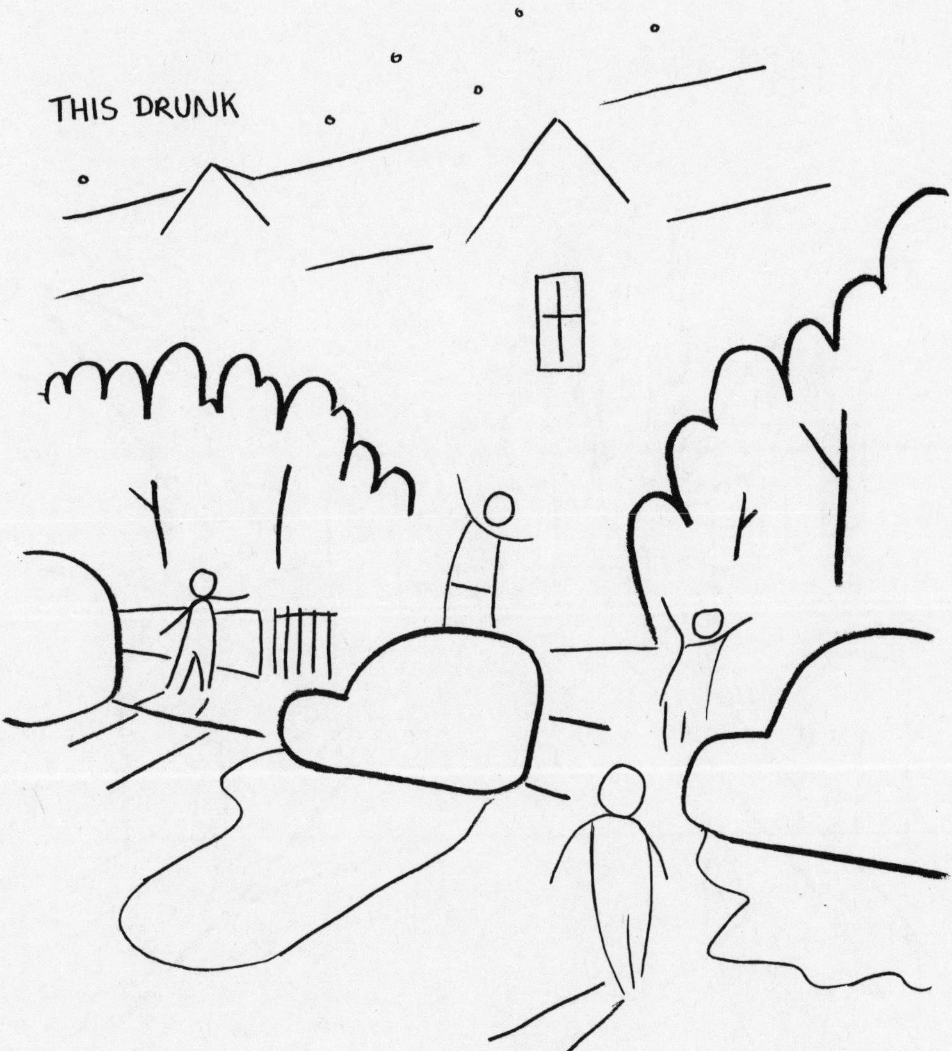
THIS DRUNK

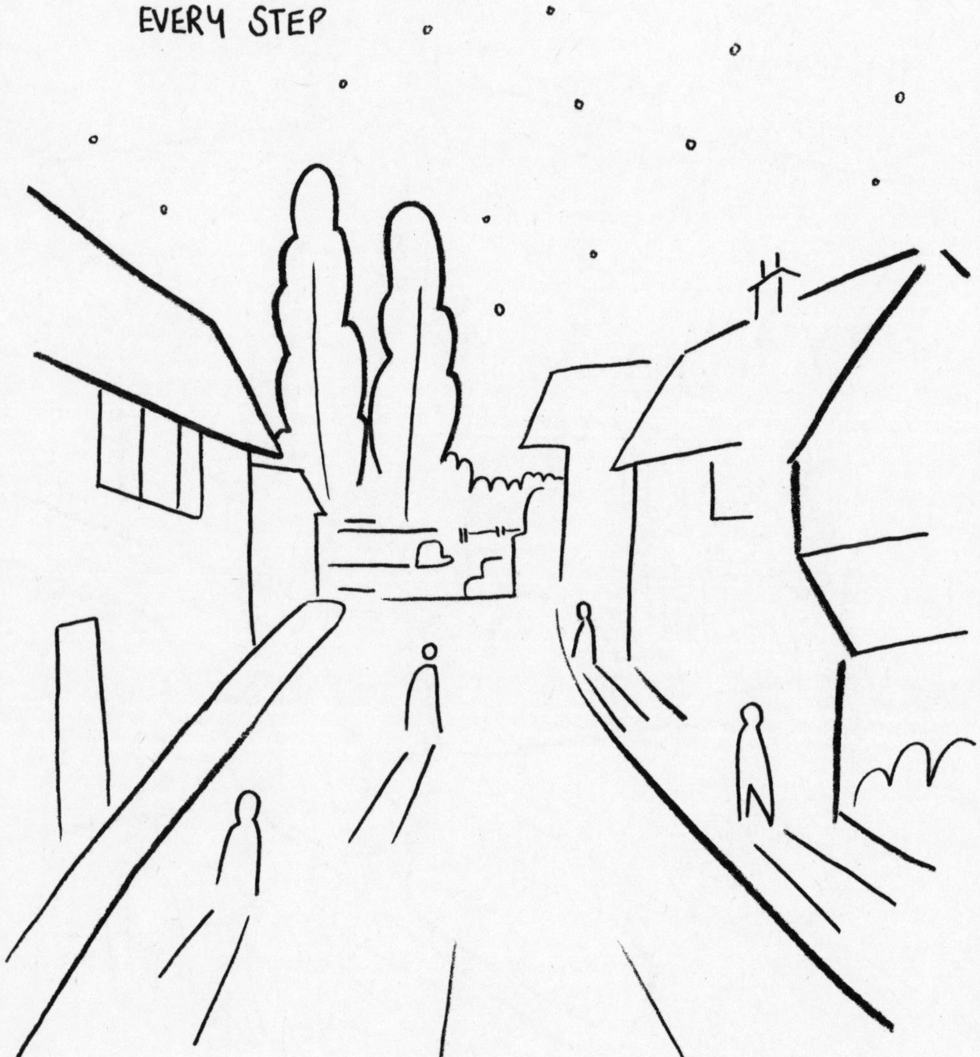
EVERY STEP

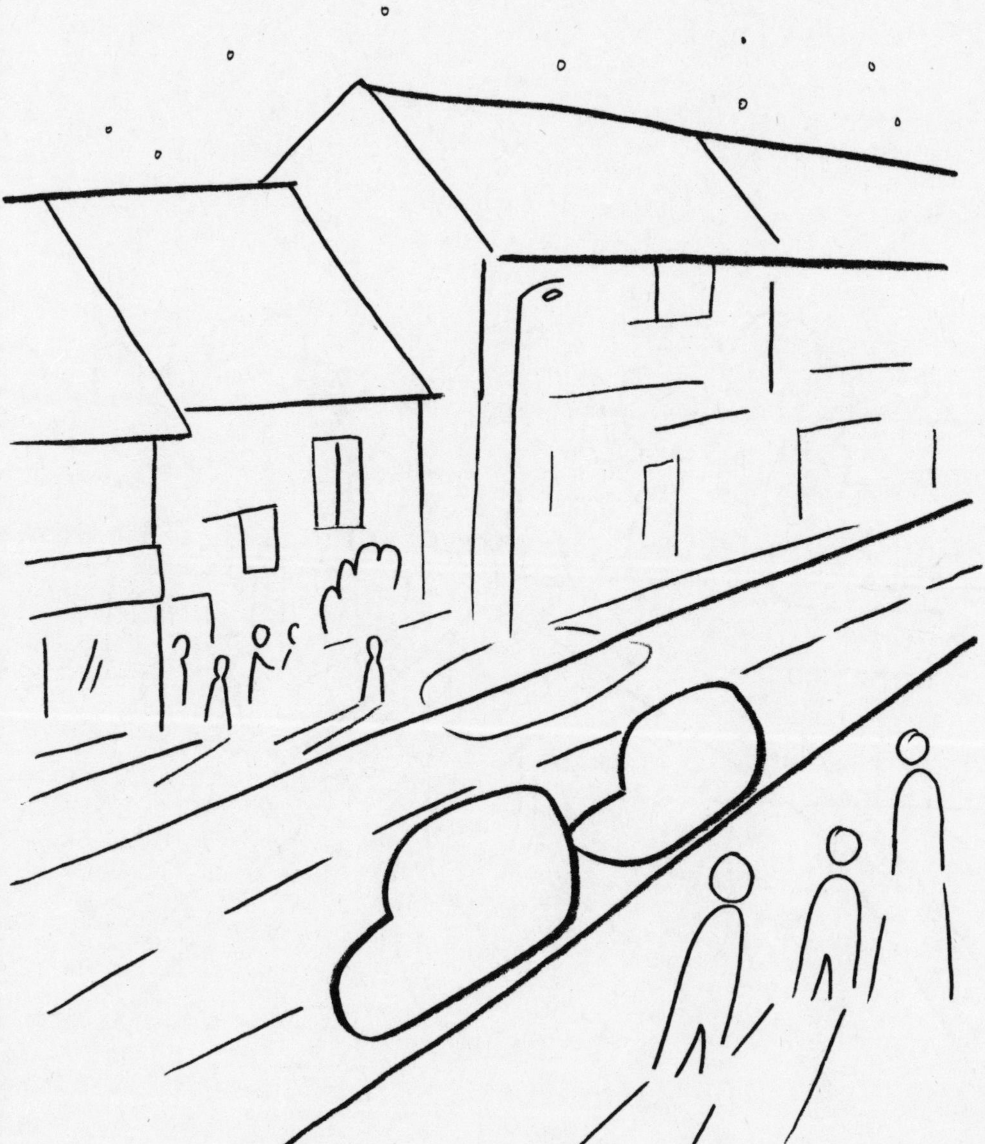

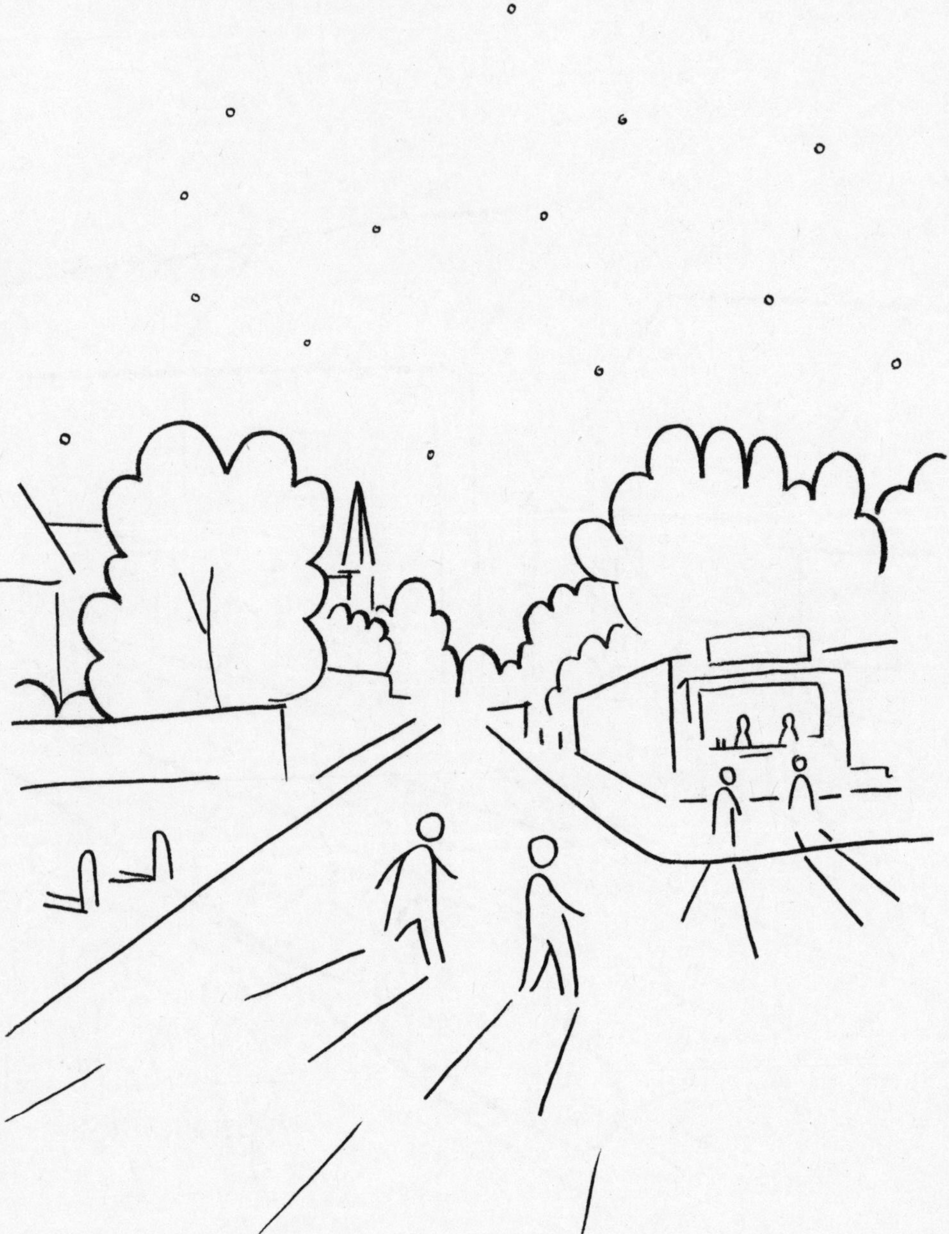

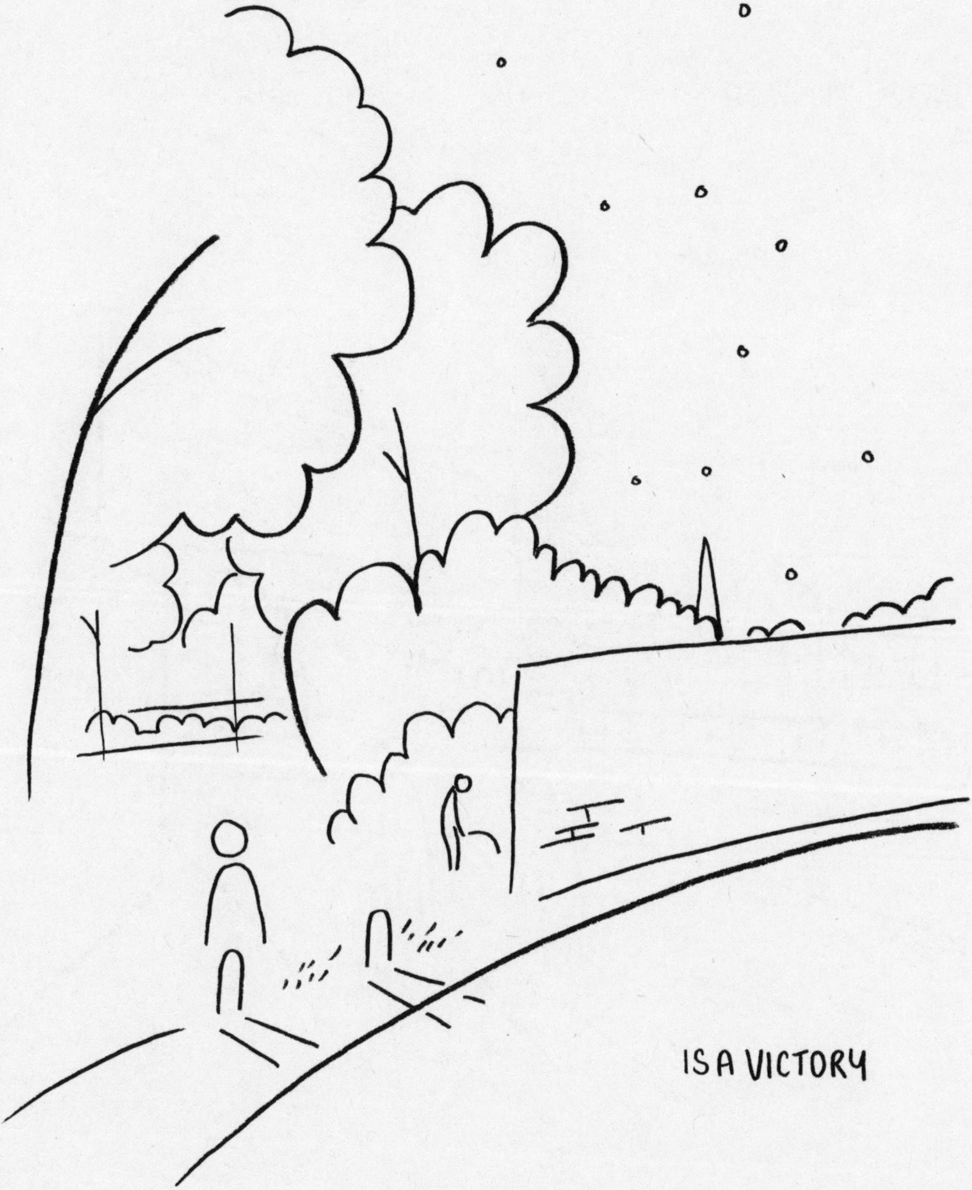
IS A VICTORY

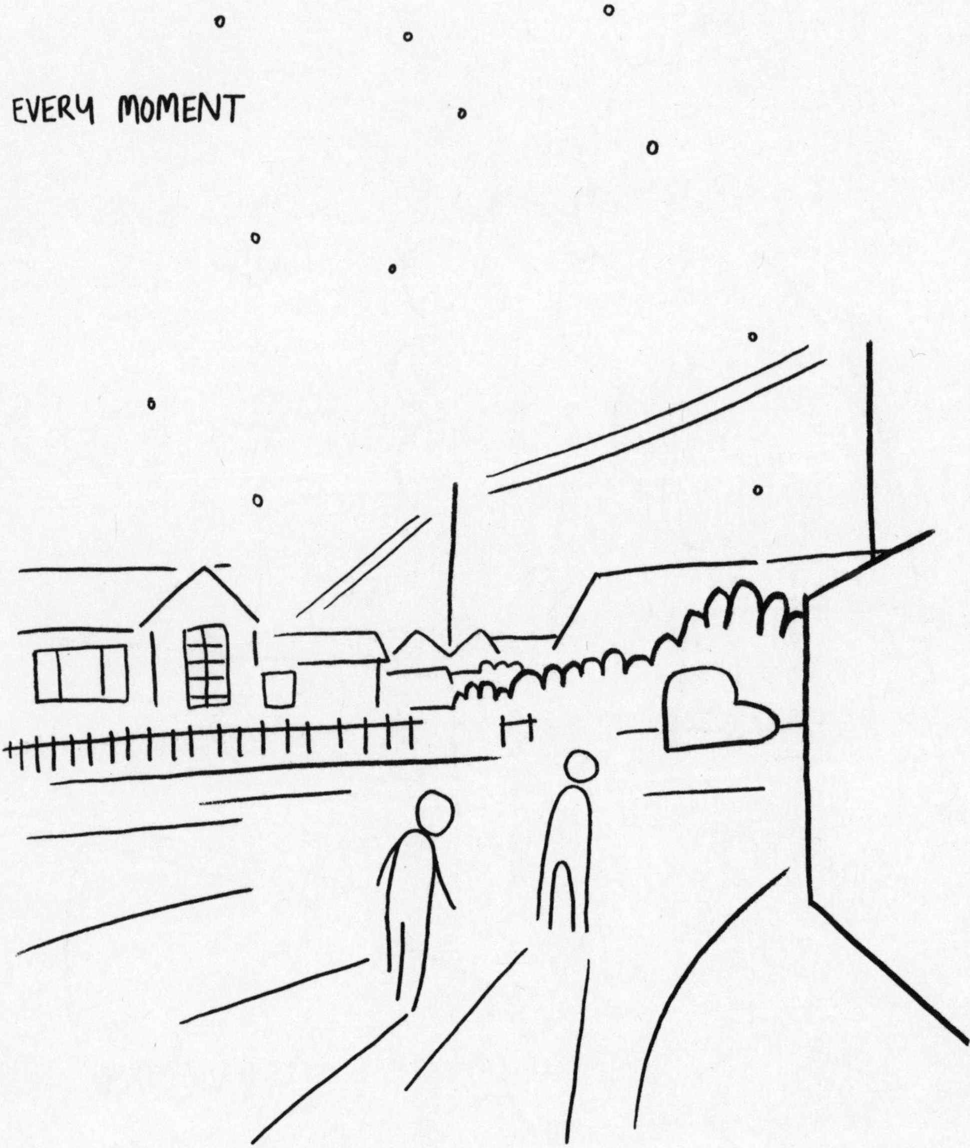
EVERY MOMENT

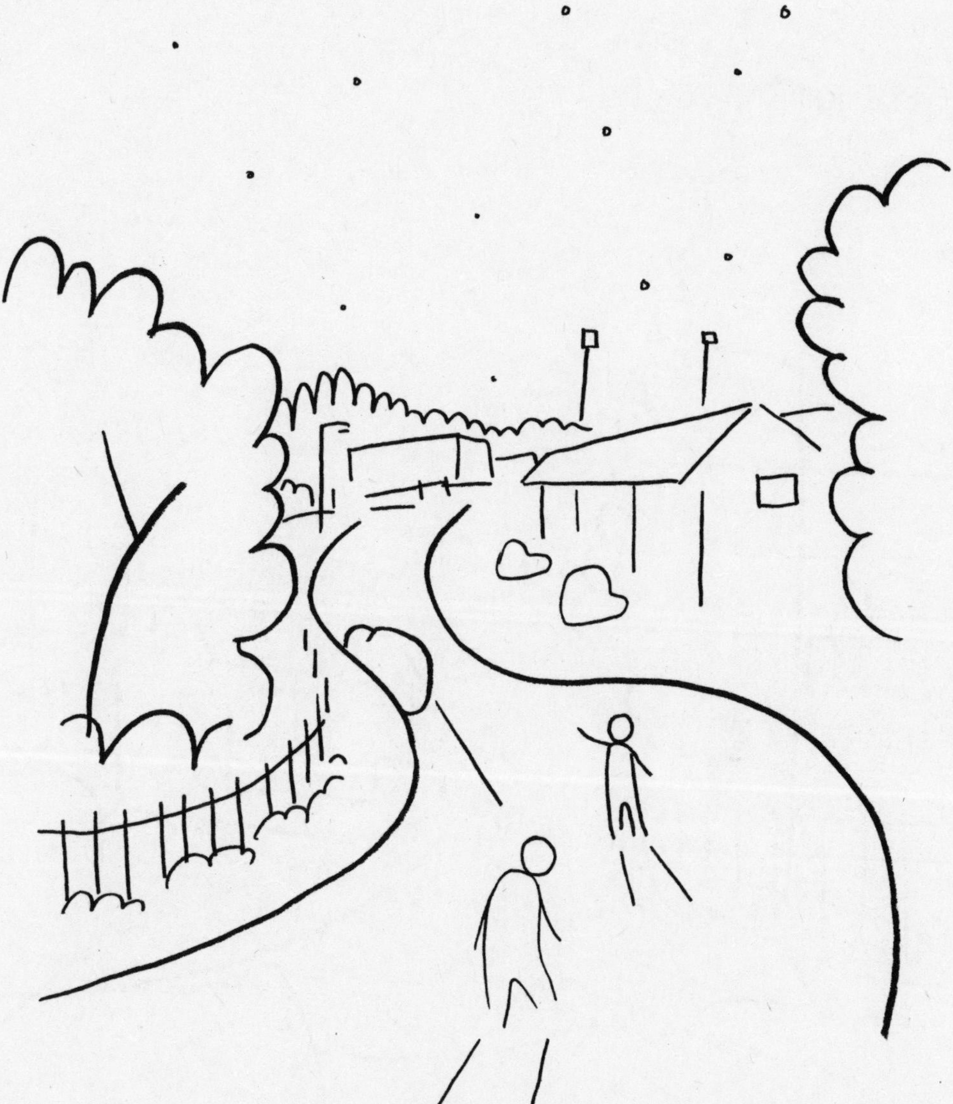

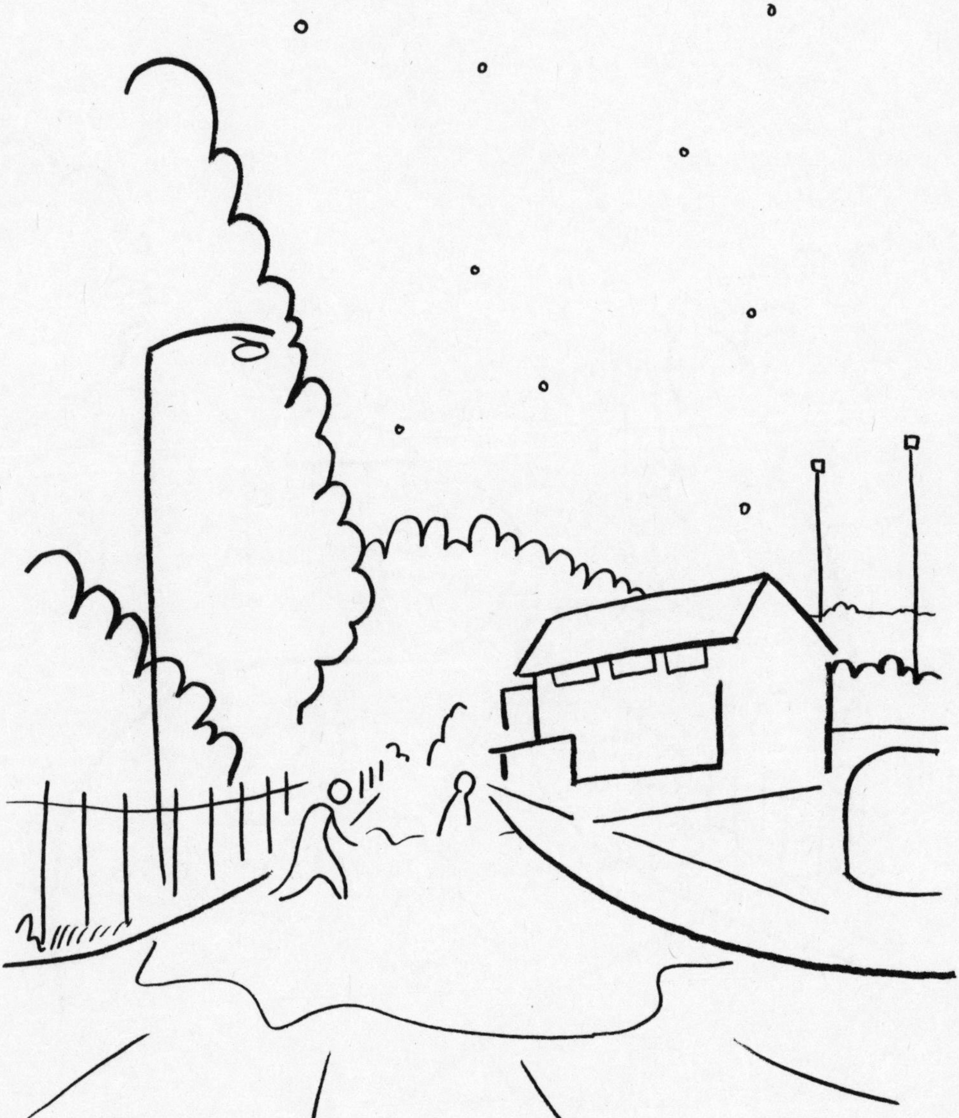

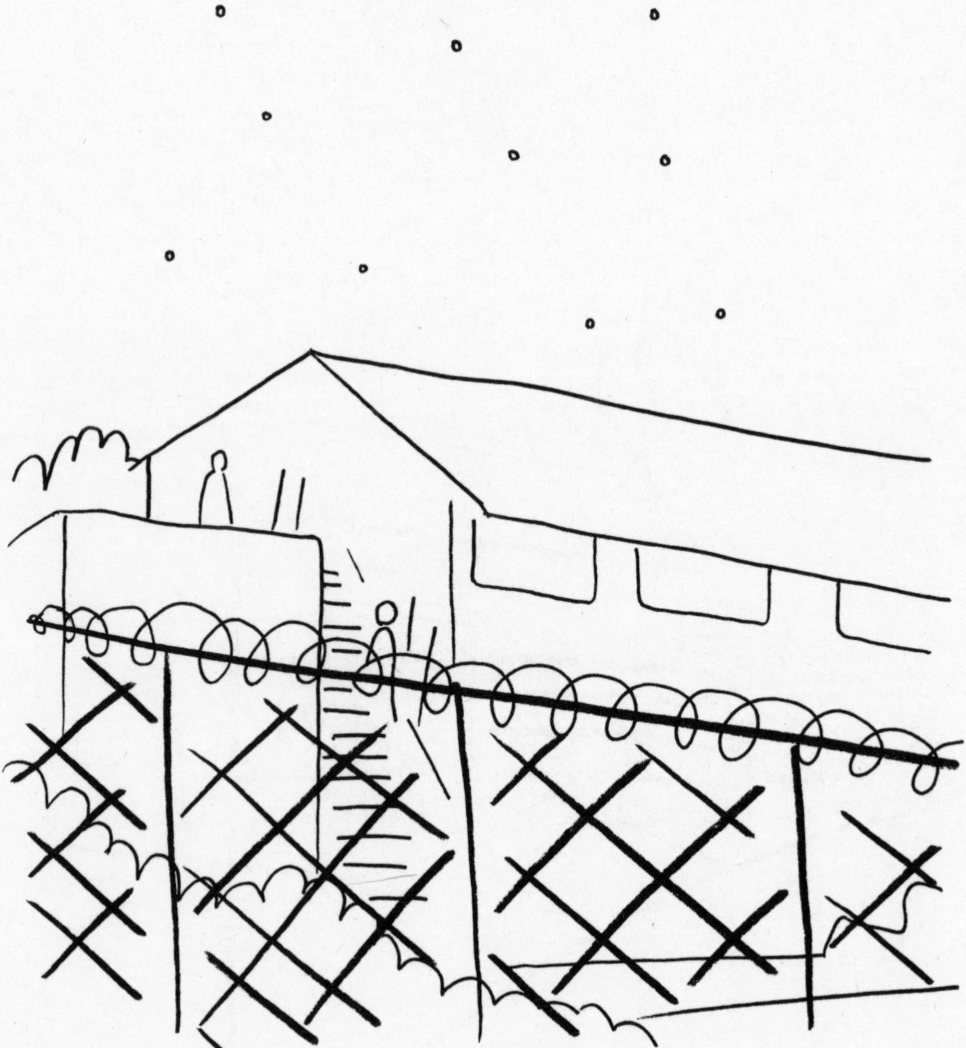

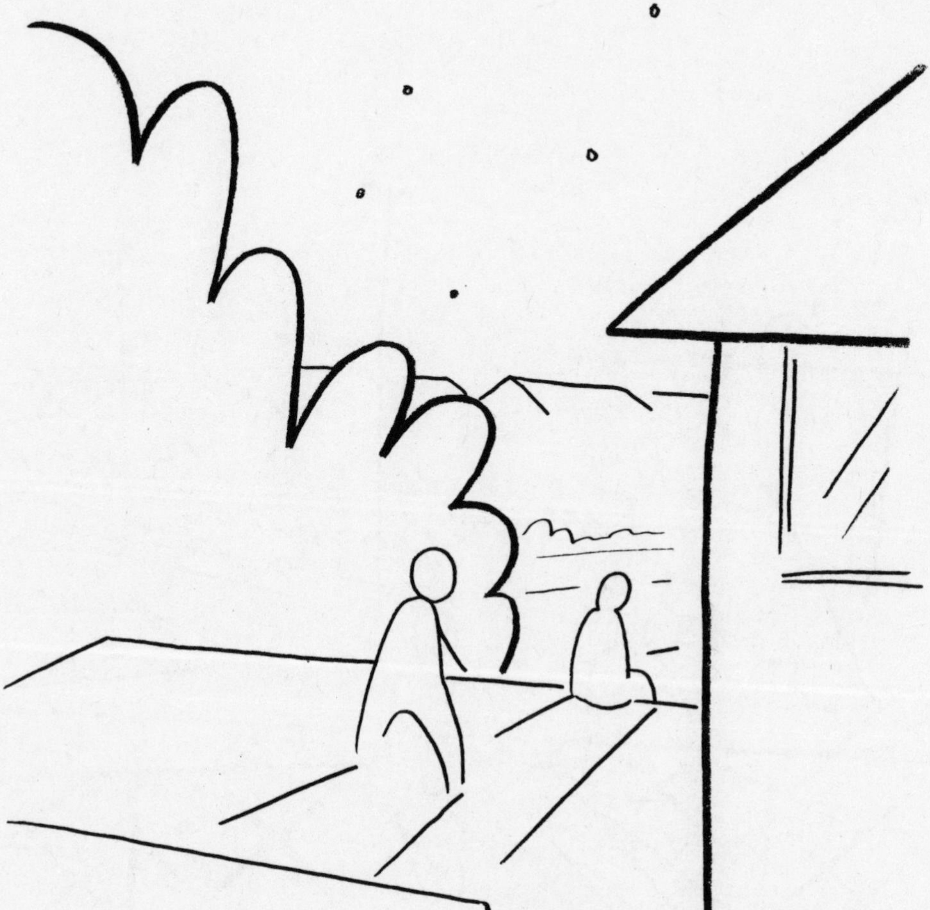

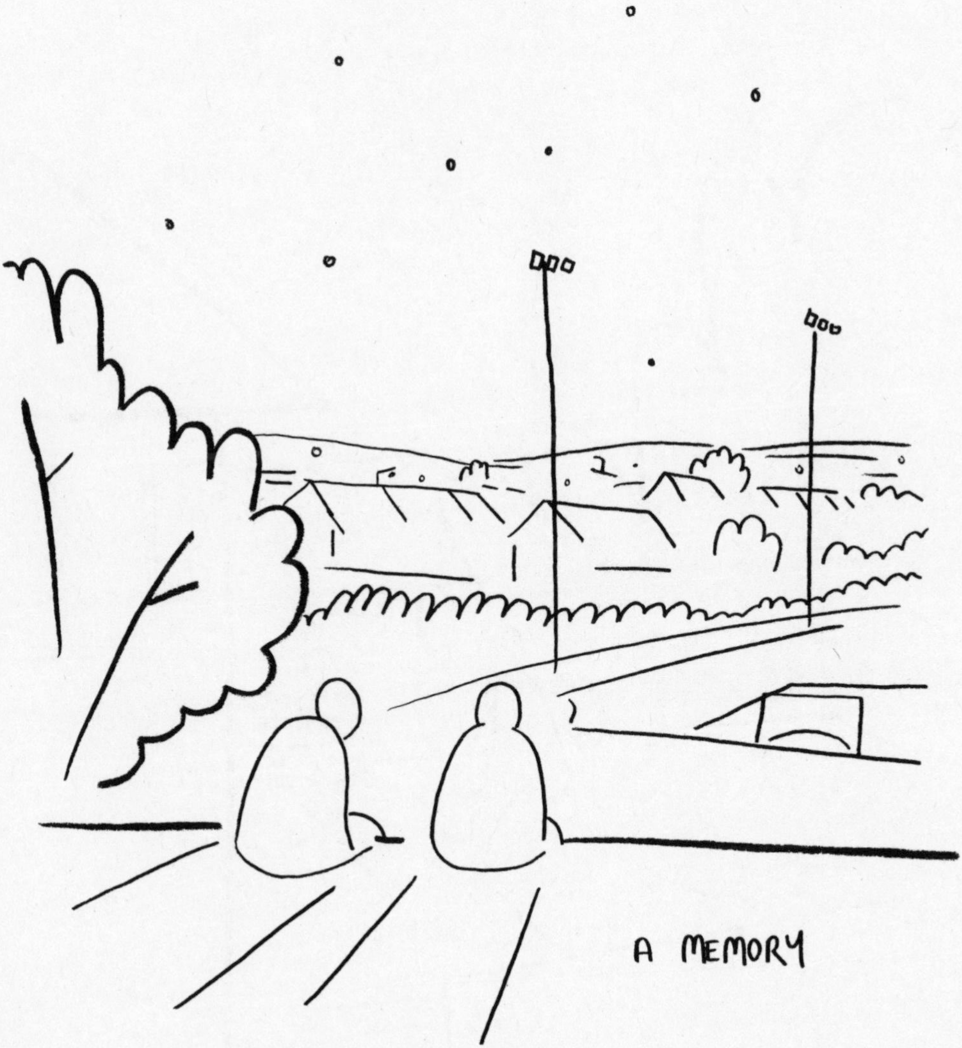
A MEMORY

THINGS WERE CHANGING

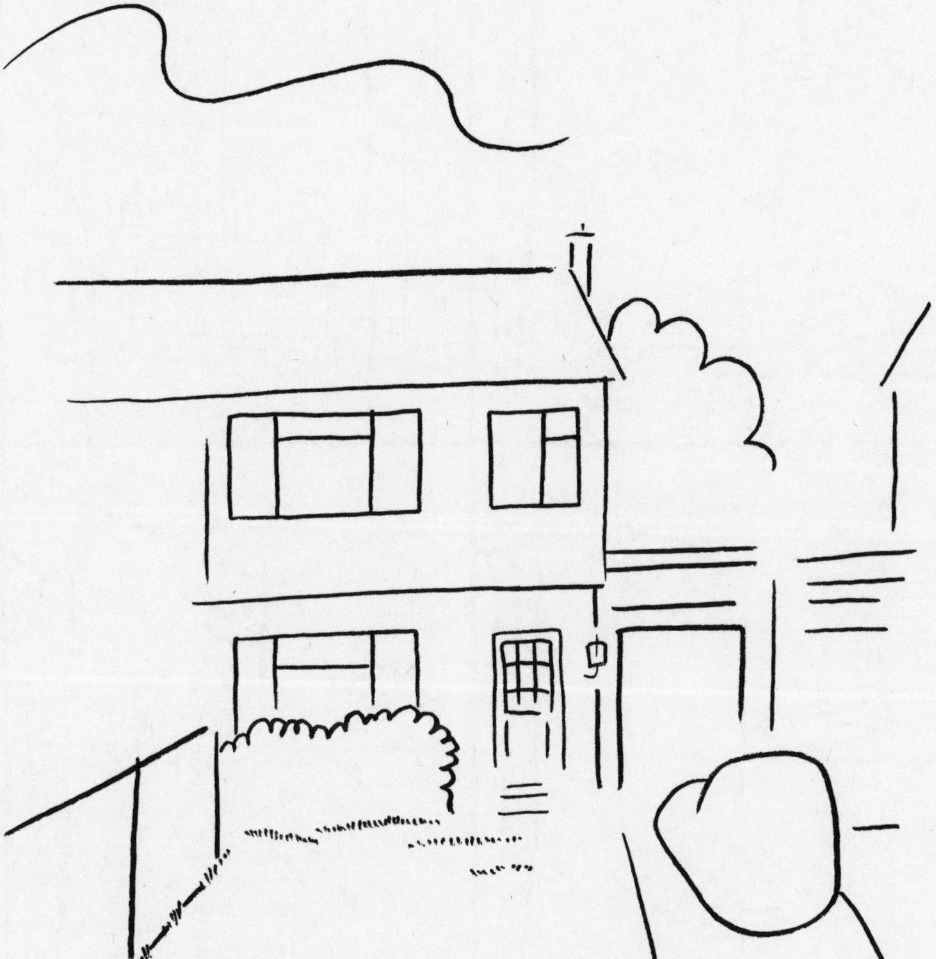

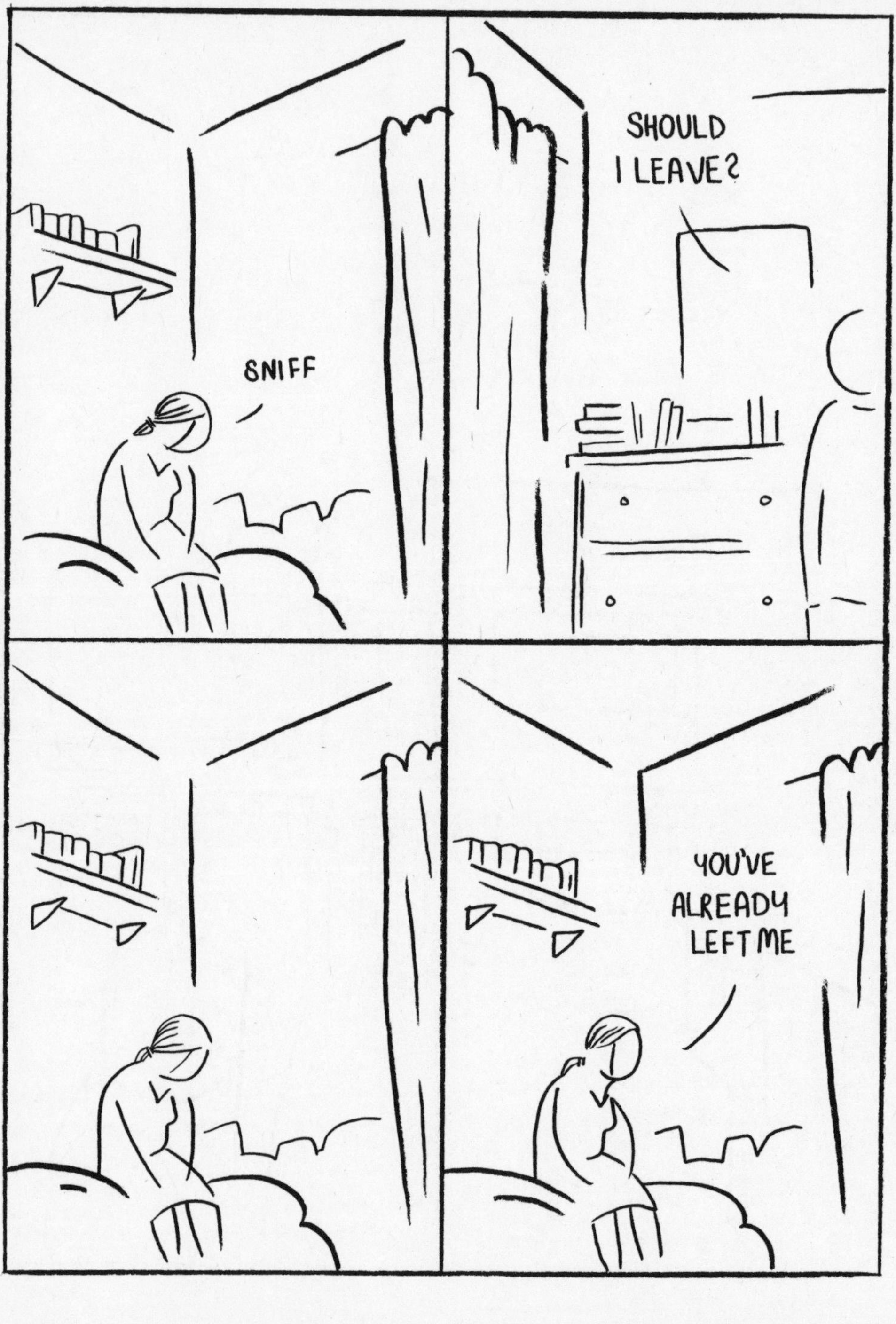
SNIFF
SHOULD I LEAVE?
YOU'VE ALREADY LEFT ME

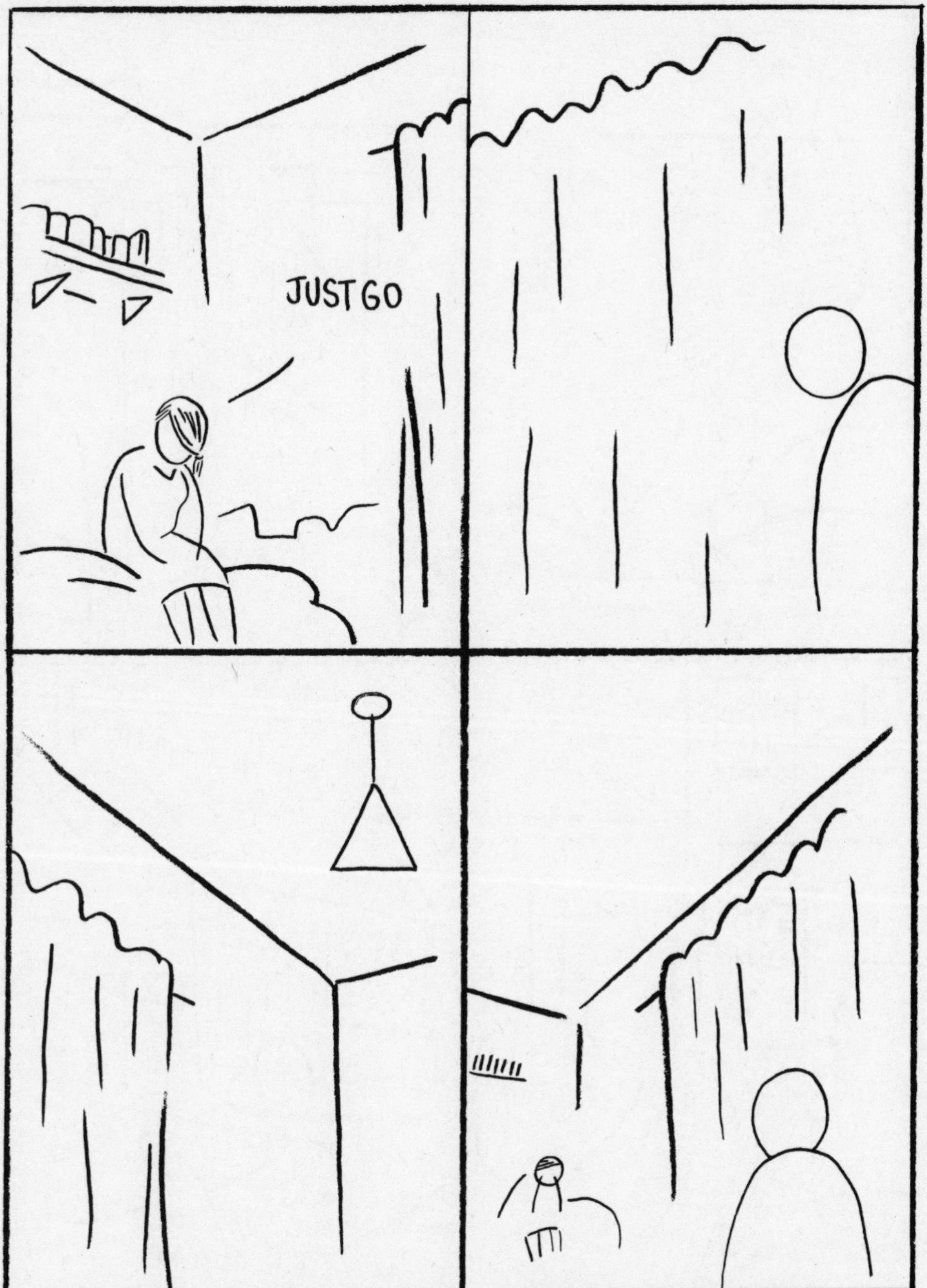
JUST GO

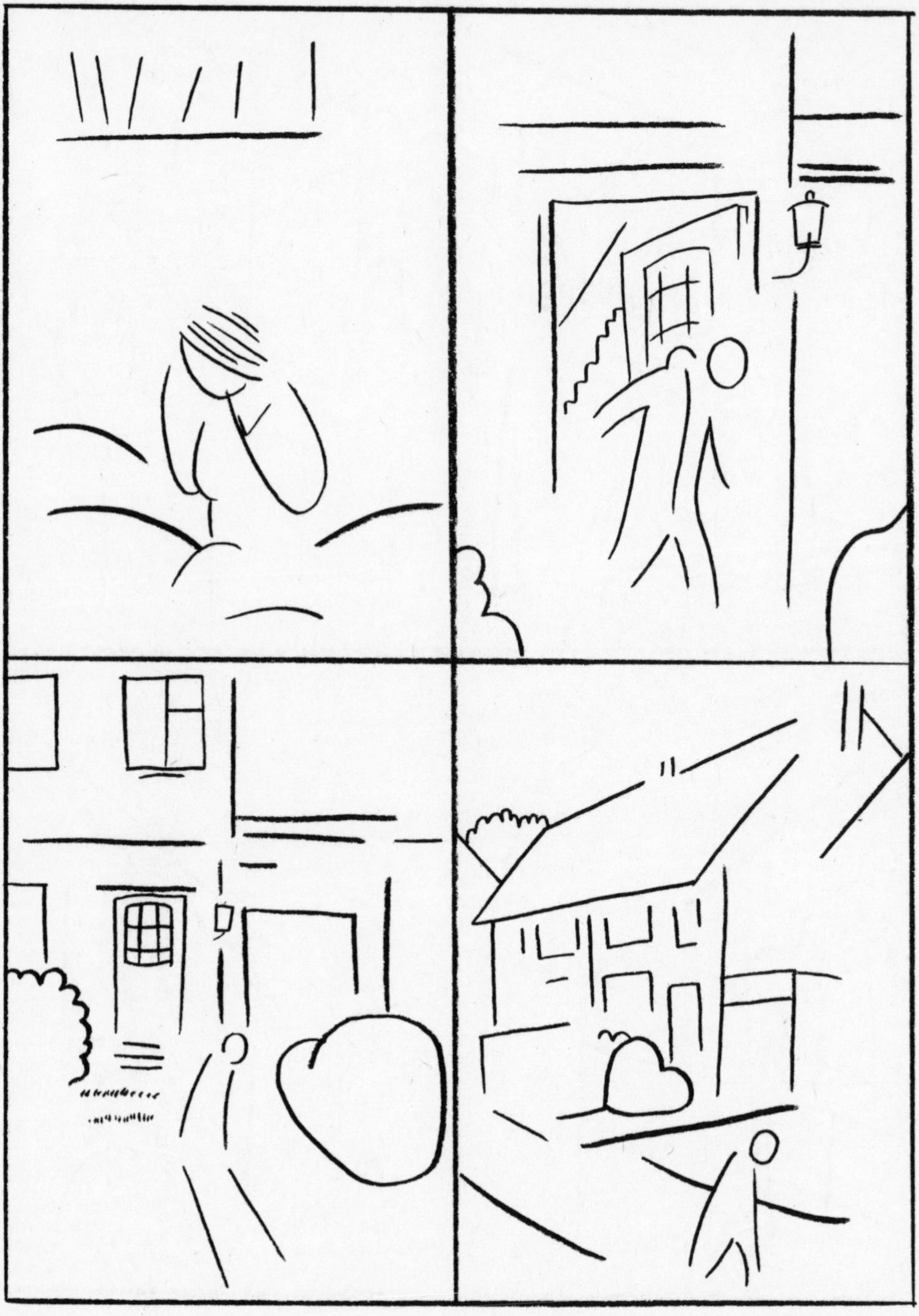

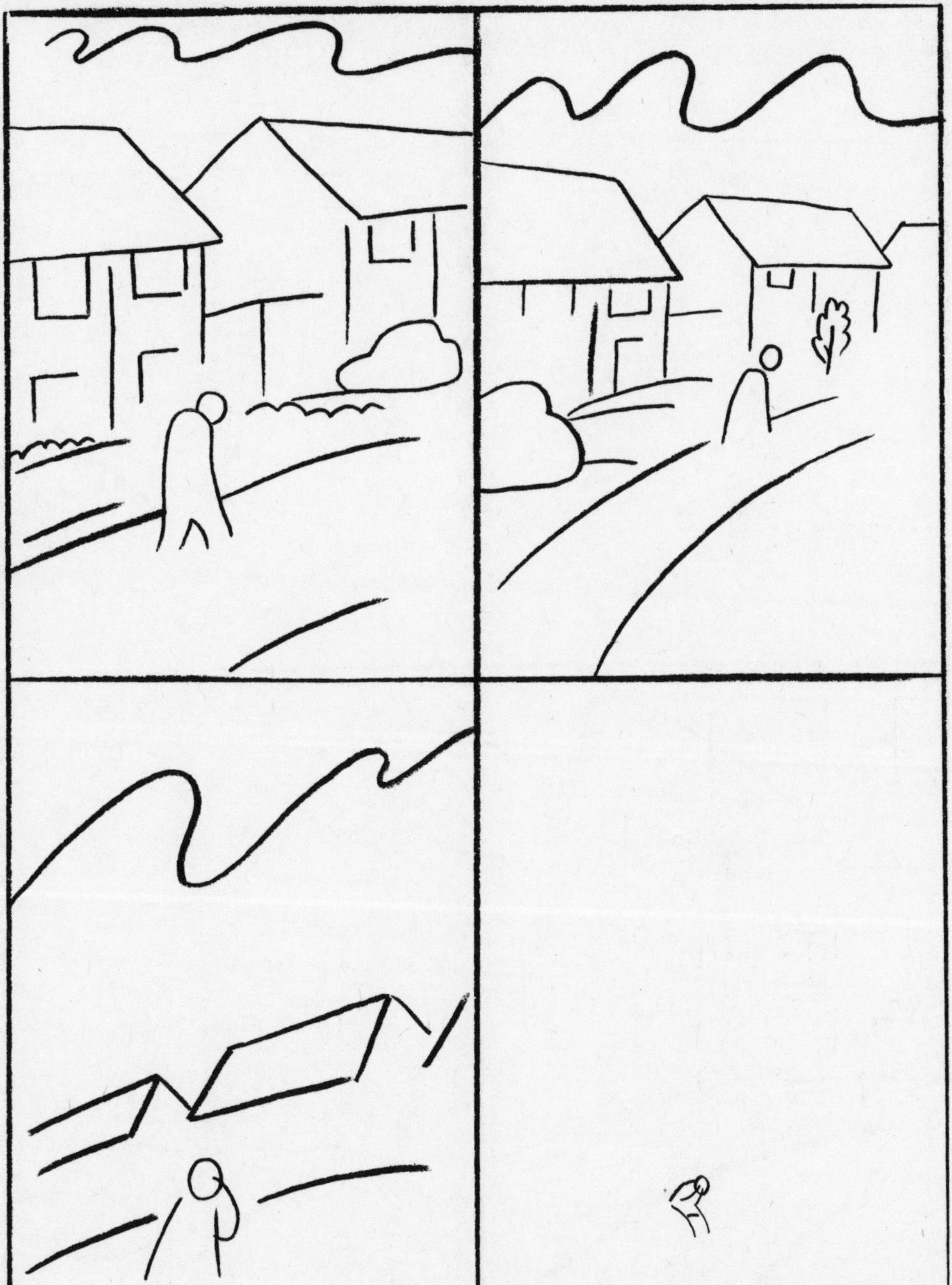

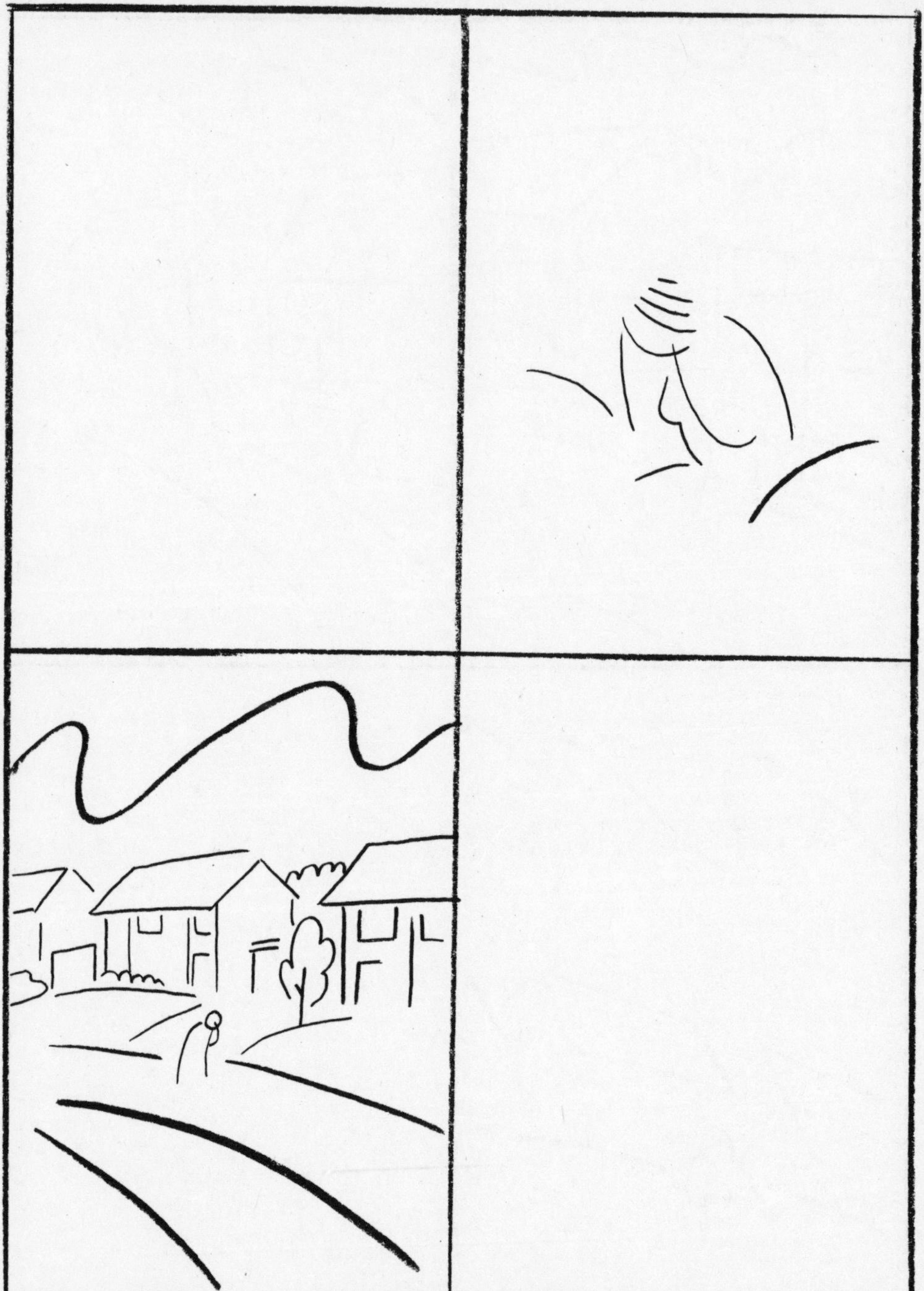

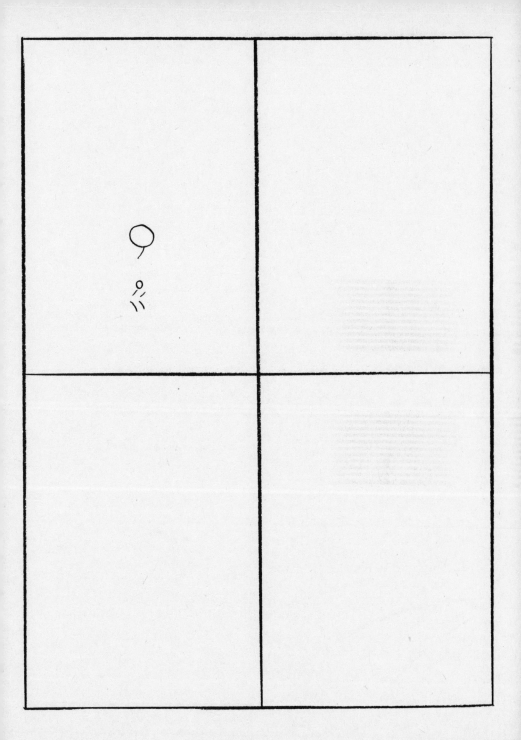

SLEEPING OUT ON THE HILL
THAT OVERLOOKS BOURNE END

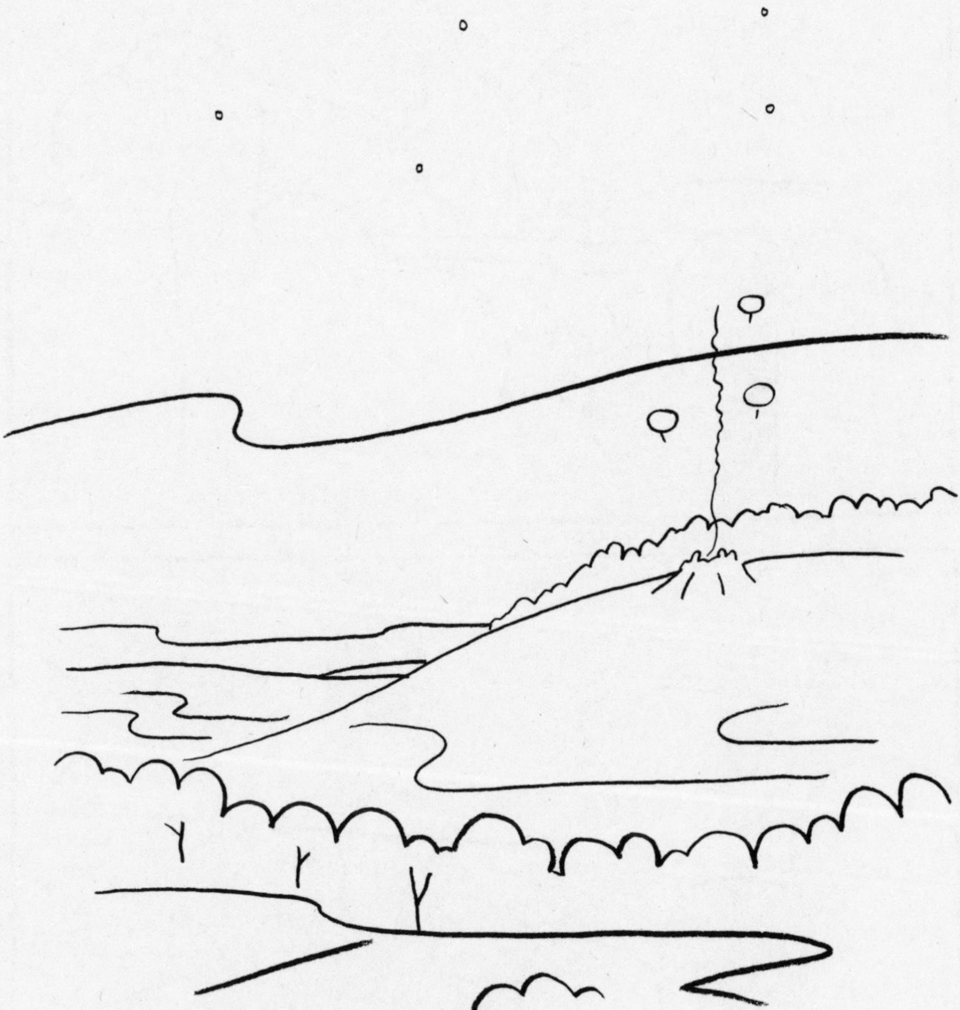

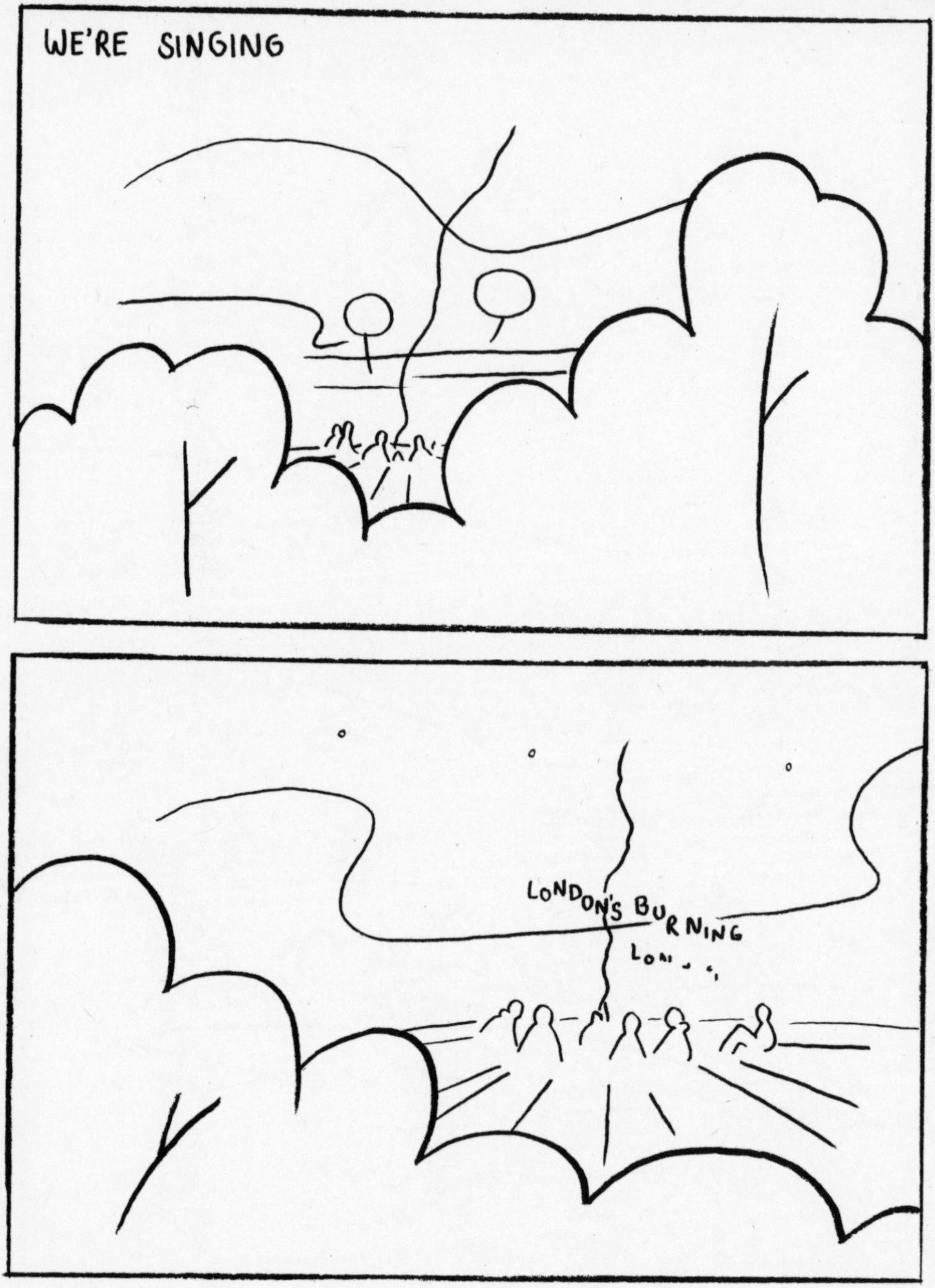
WE'RE SINGING
LONDON'S BURNING
LON

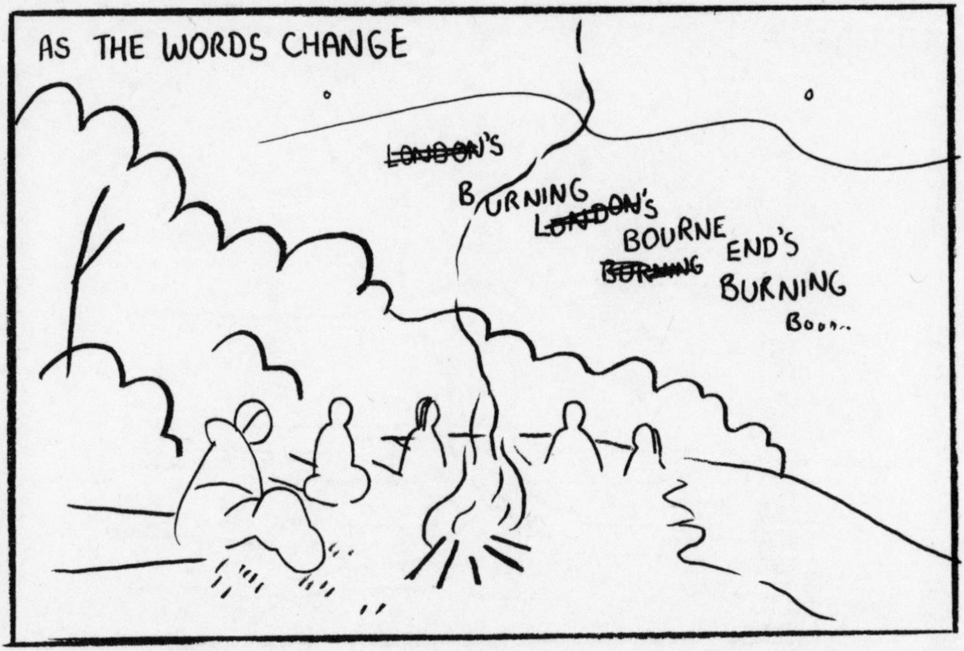
AS THE WORDS CHANGE
~~LONDON~~'S
BURNING
~~LONDON~~'S
BOURNE
~~BURNING~~
END'S
BURNING
Boo..

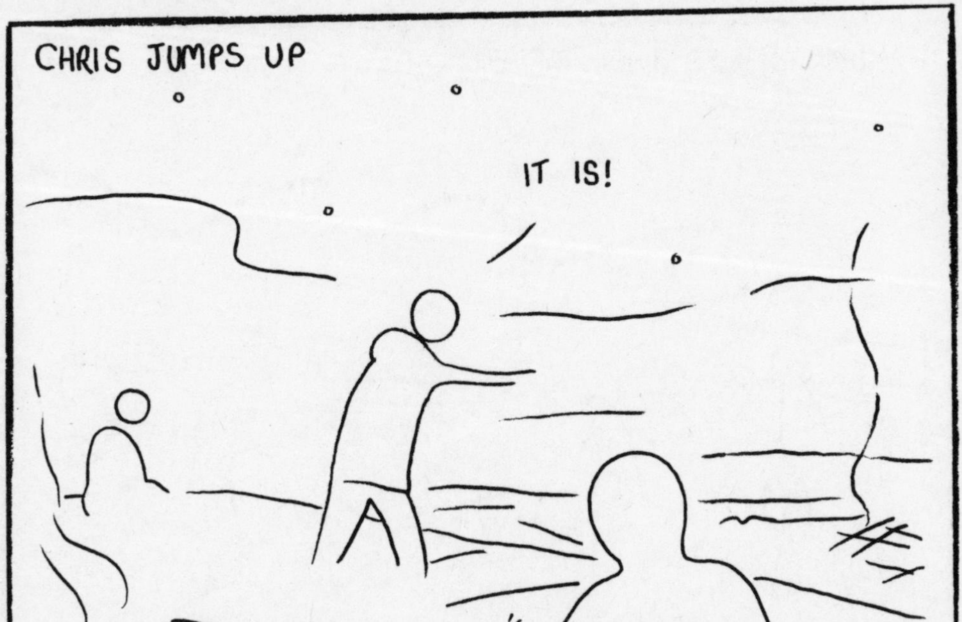
CHRIS JUMPS UP
IT IS!

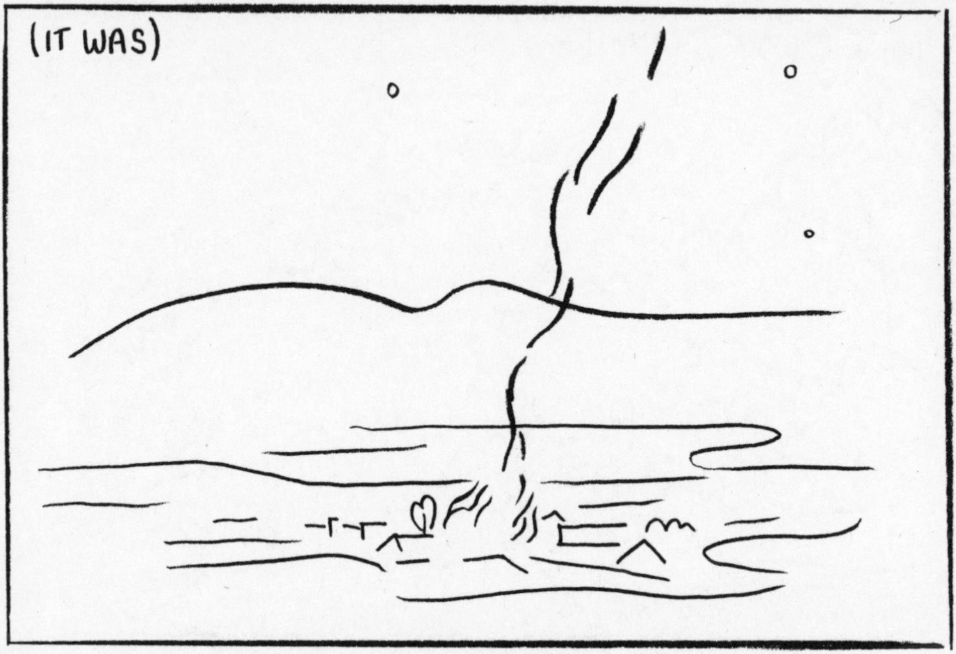
(IT WAS)

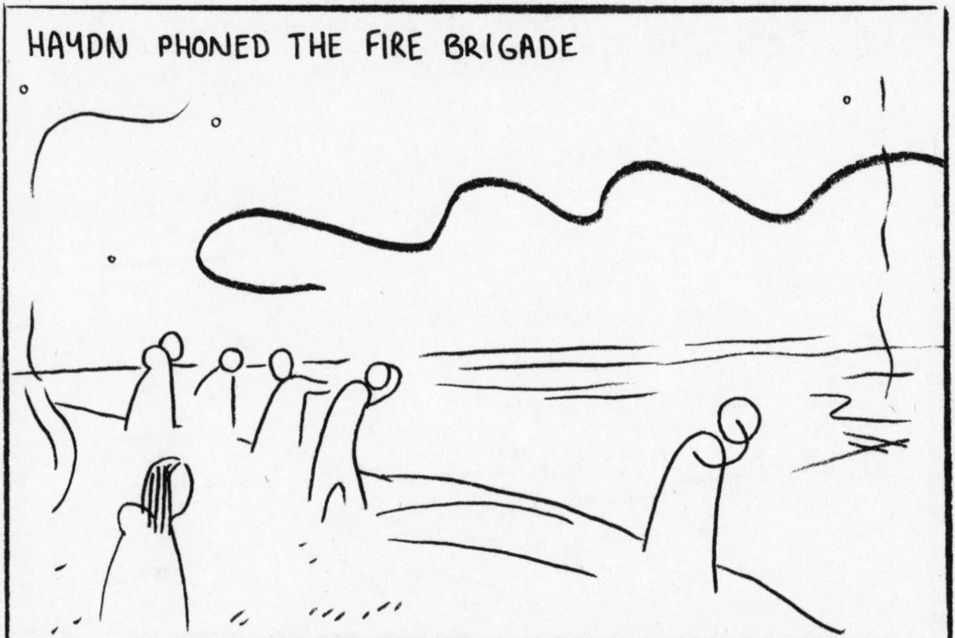
HAYDN PHONED THE FIRE BRIGADE

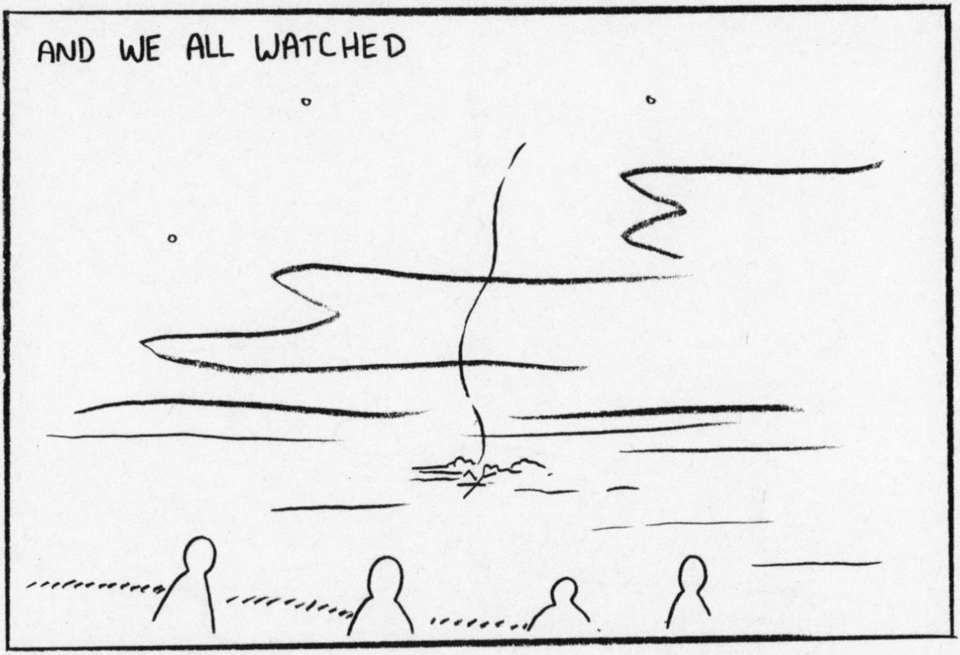
AND WE ALL WATCHED

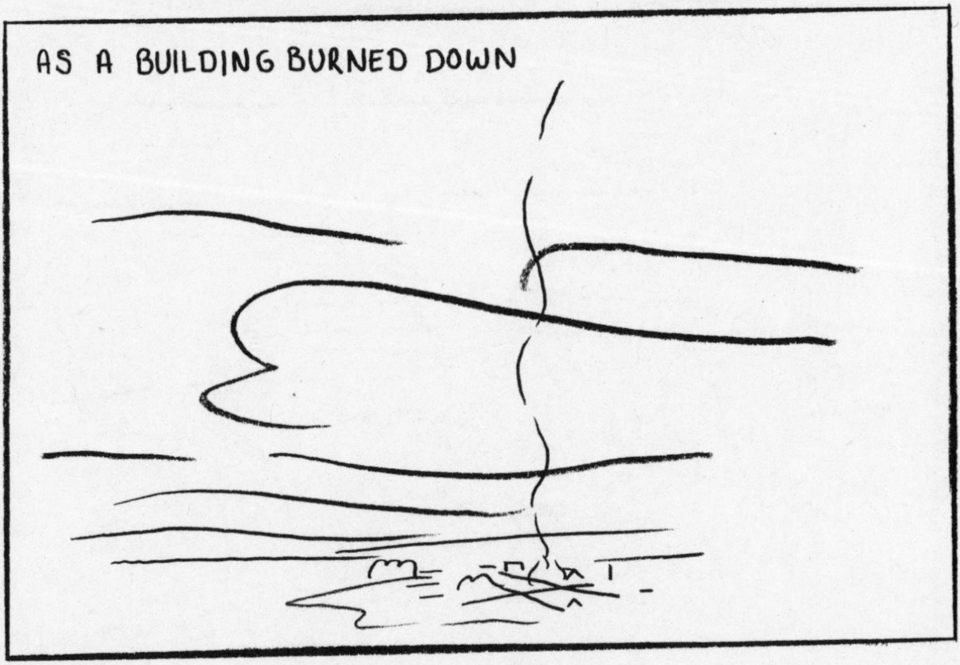
AS A BUILDING BURNED DOWN

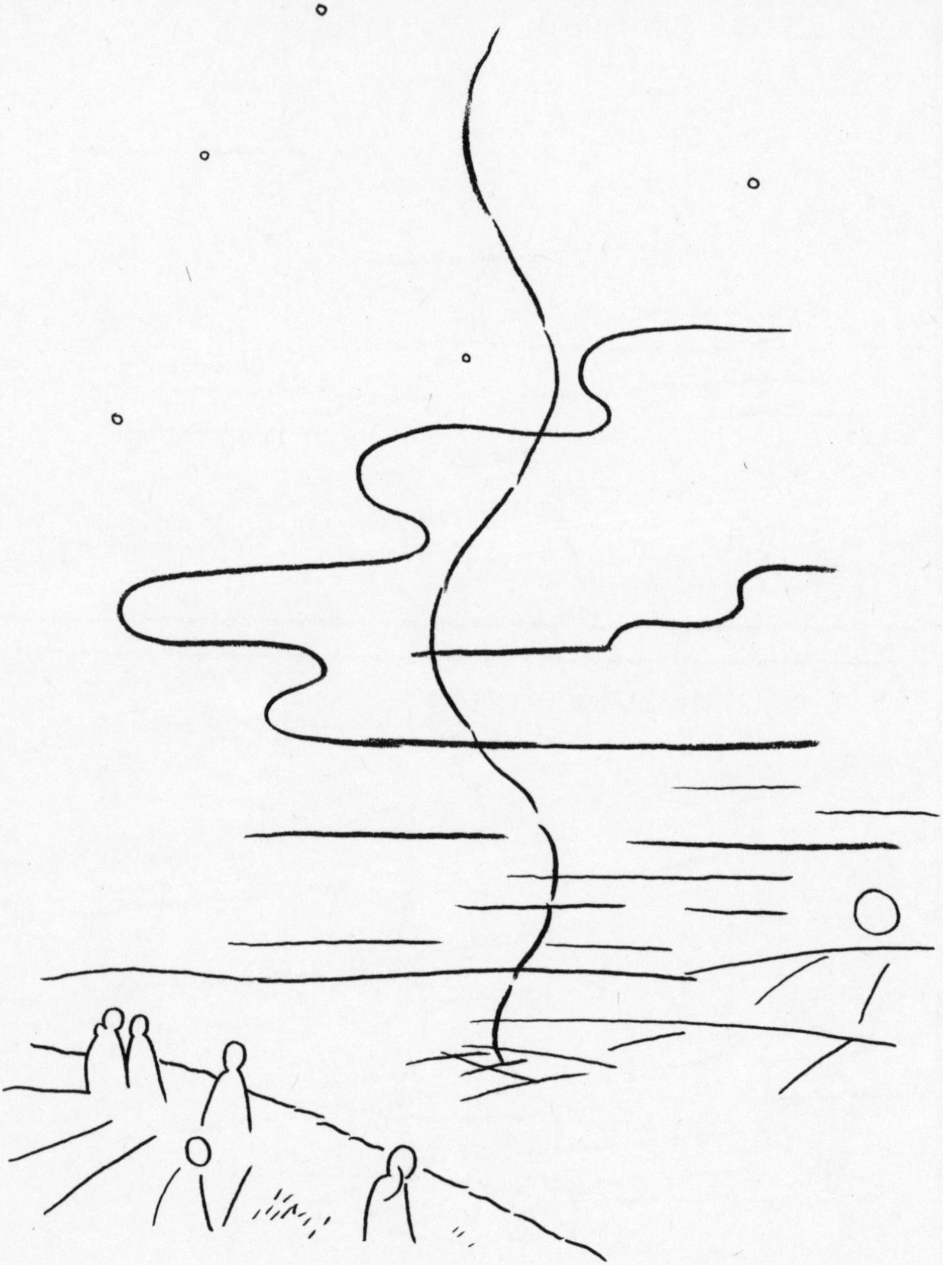

AND THE SUN CAME UP

DURING THAT FINAL SEPTEMBER
MY PARENTS WENT AWAY

I WAS HOME ALONE

I LISTENED TO DAD'S RECORDS

WROTE AWFUL SONGS

SMOKED IN THE GARDEN

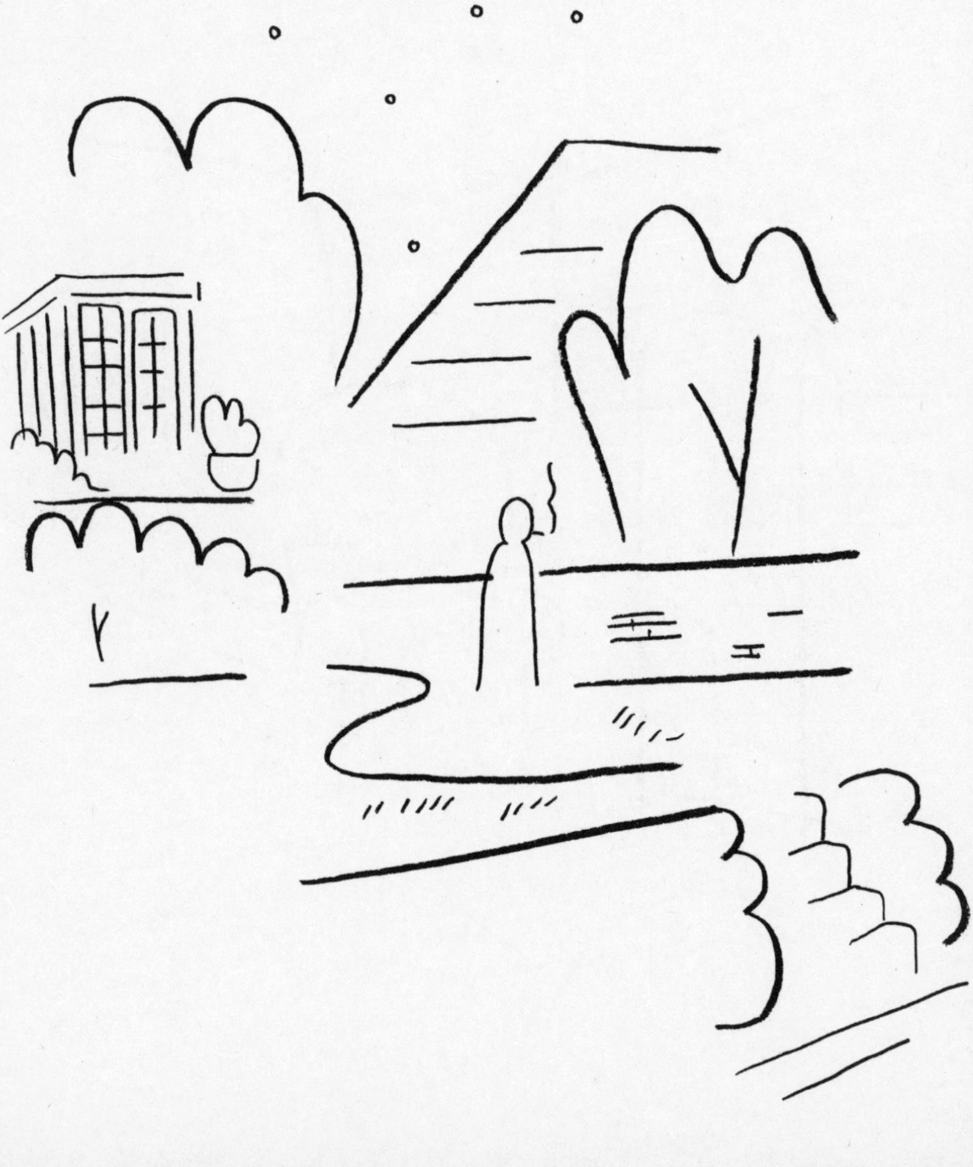

THOUGHT A LOT

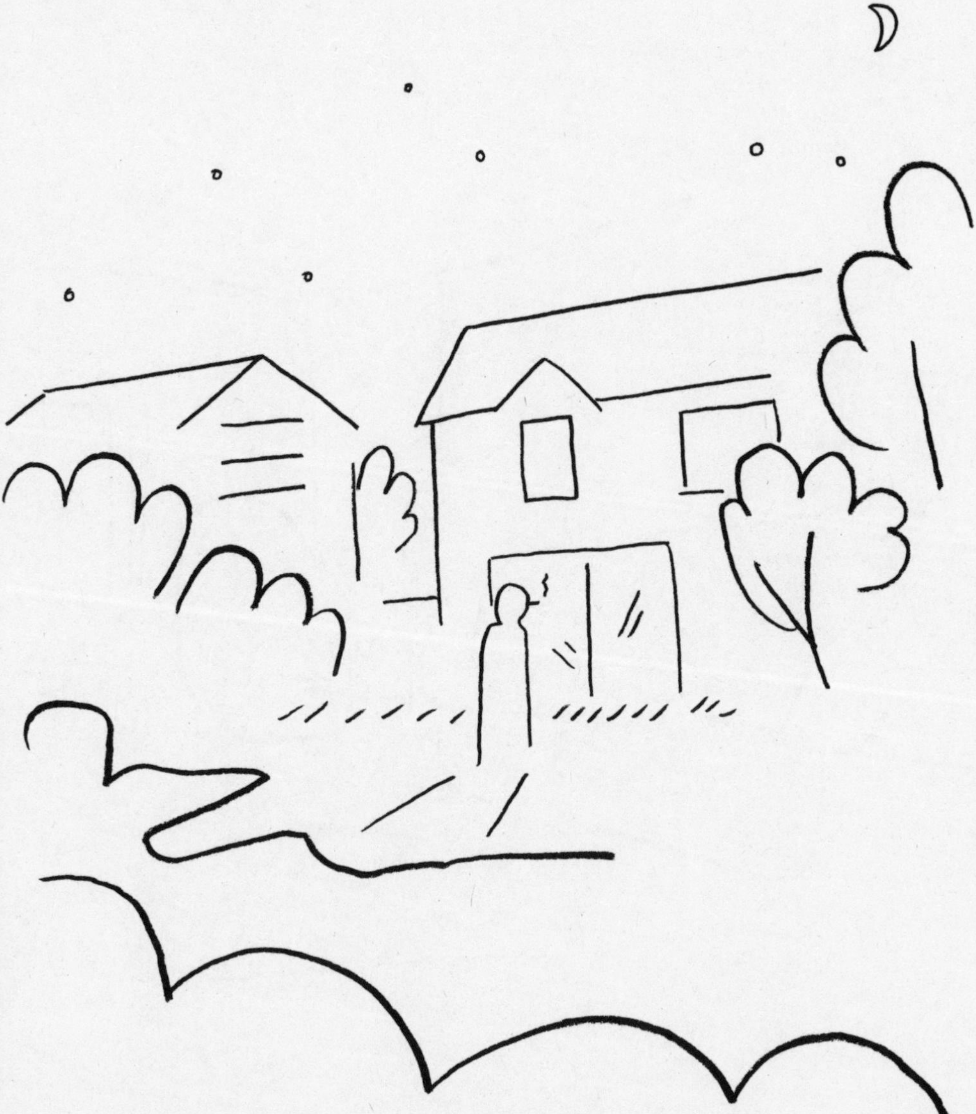

WATCHED THE NEWS

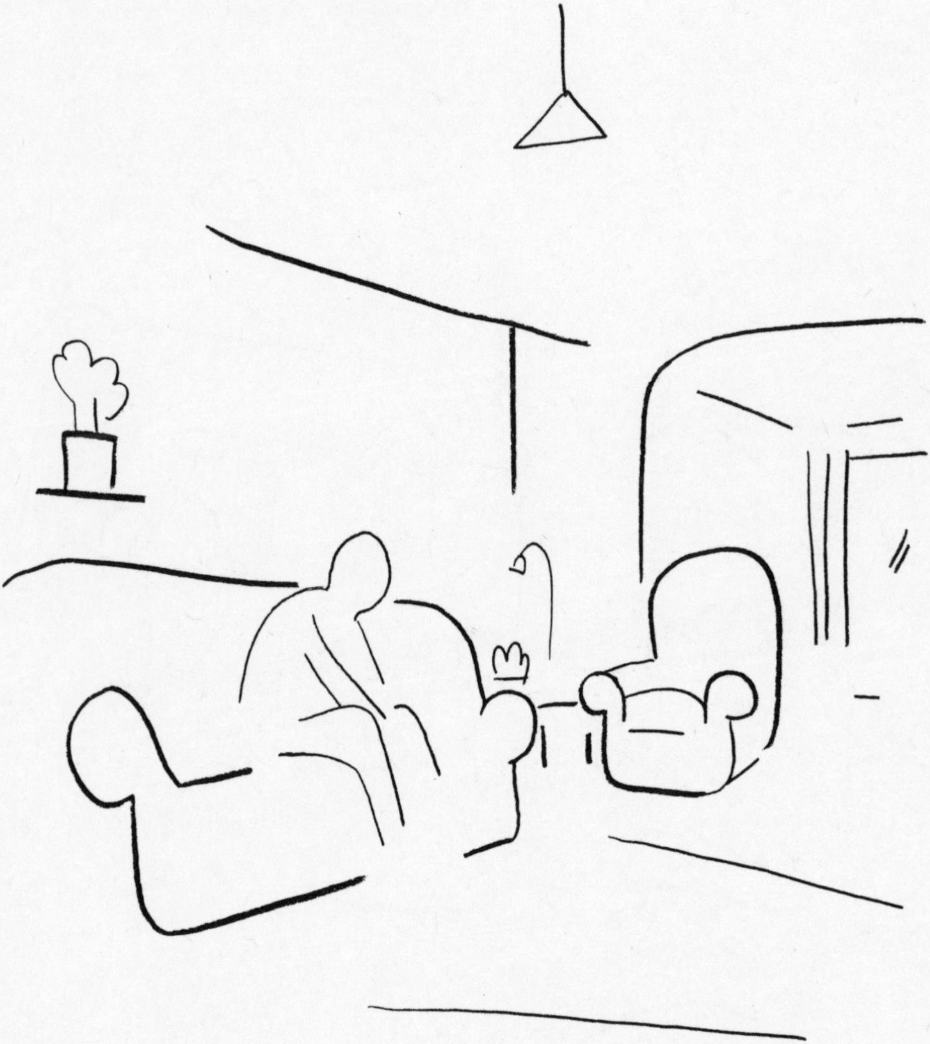

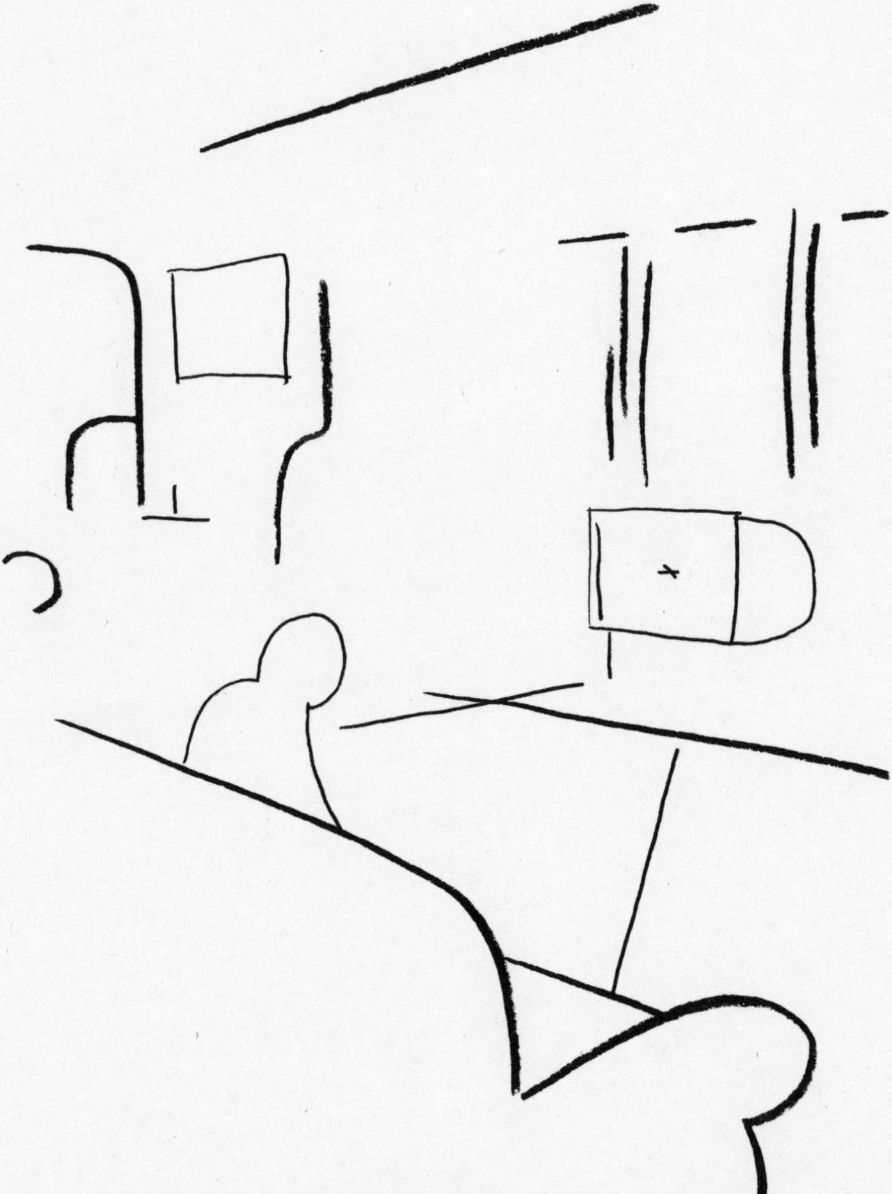

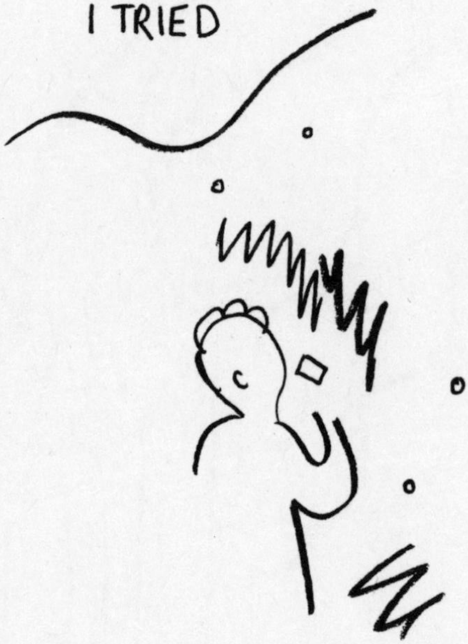
I TRIED

TO PUT IT ALL TOGETHER

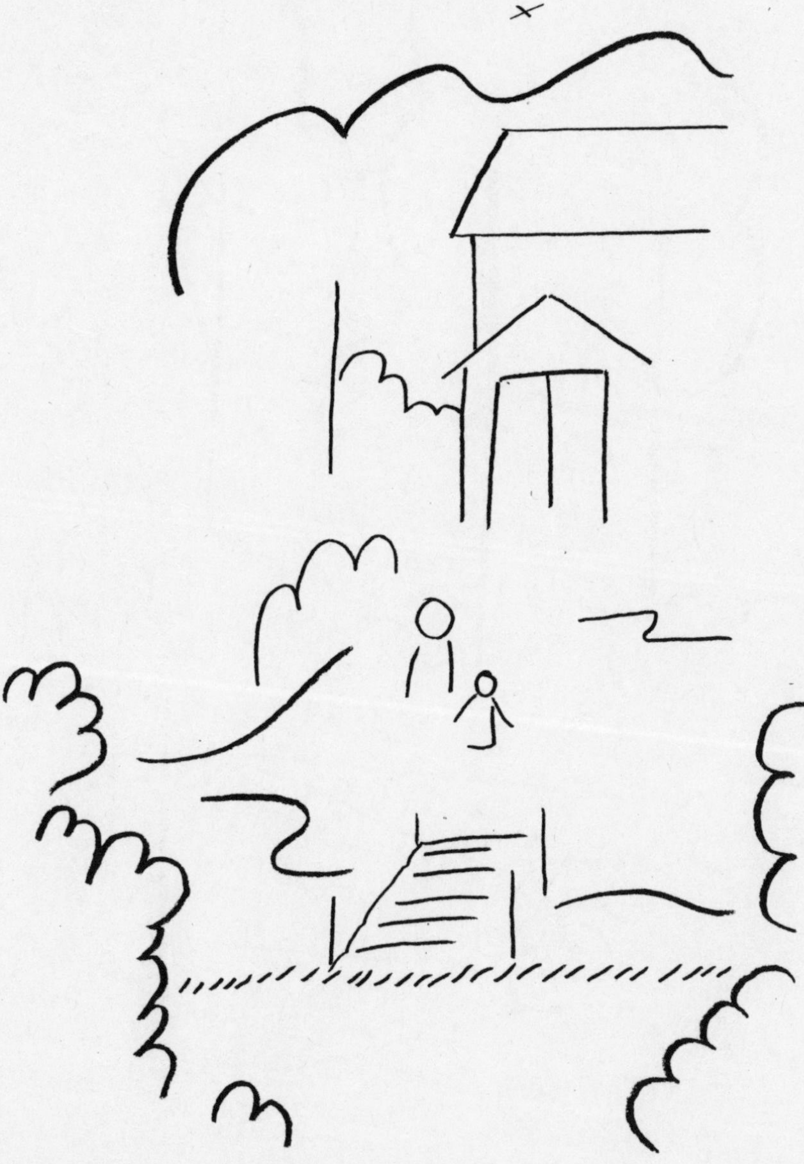

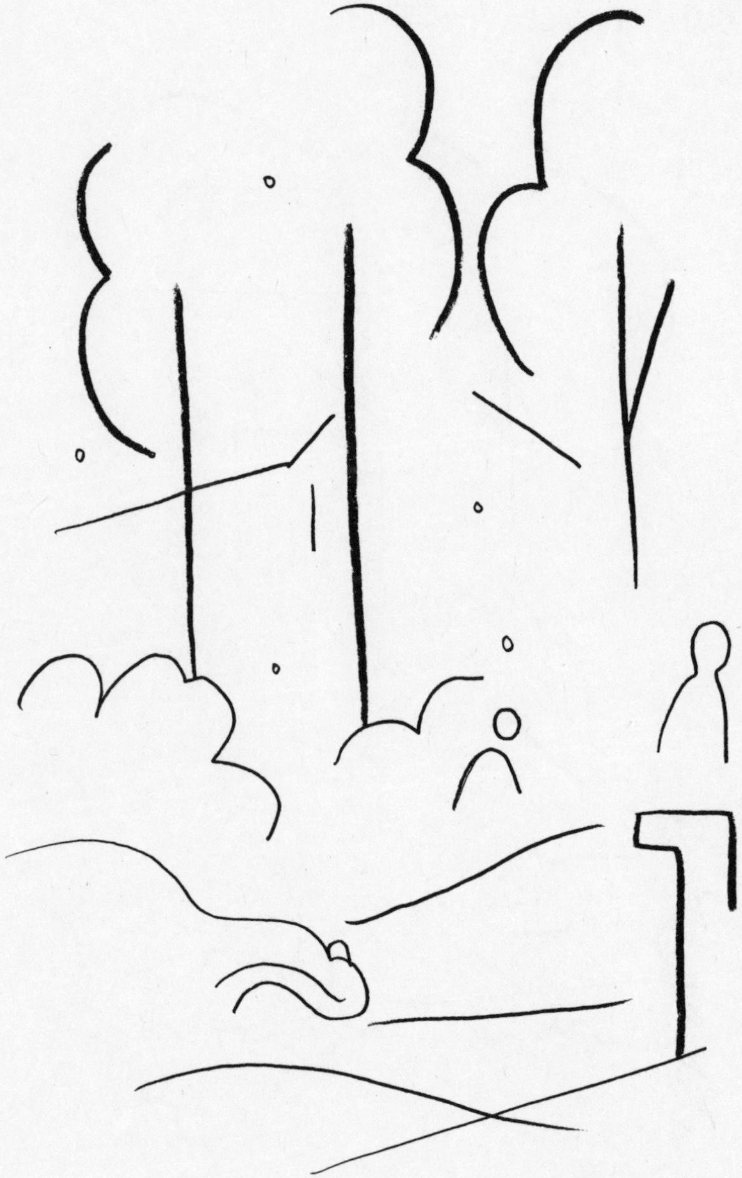

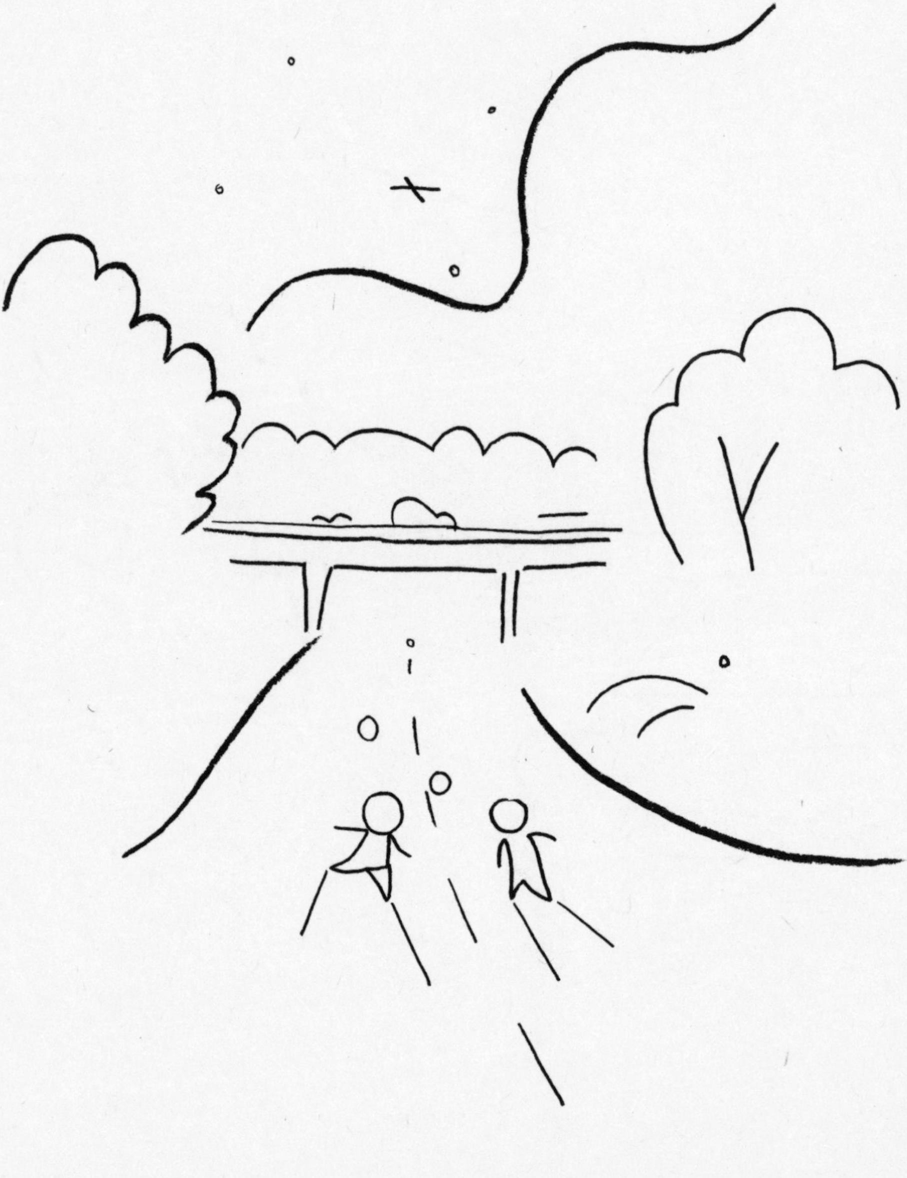

BUT IT WOULDN'T FIT

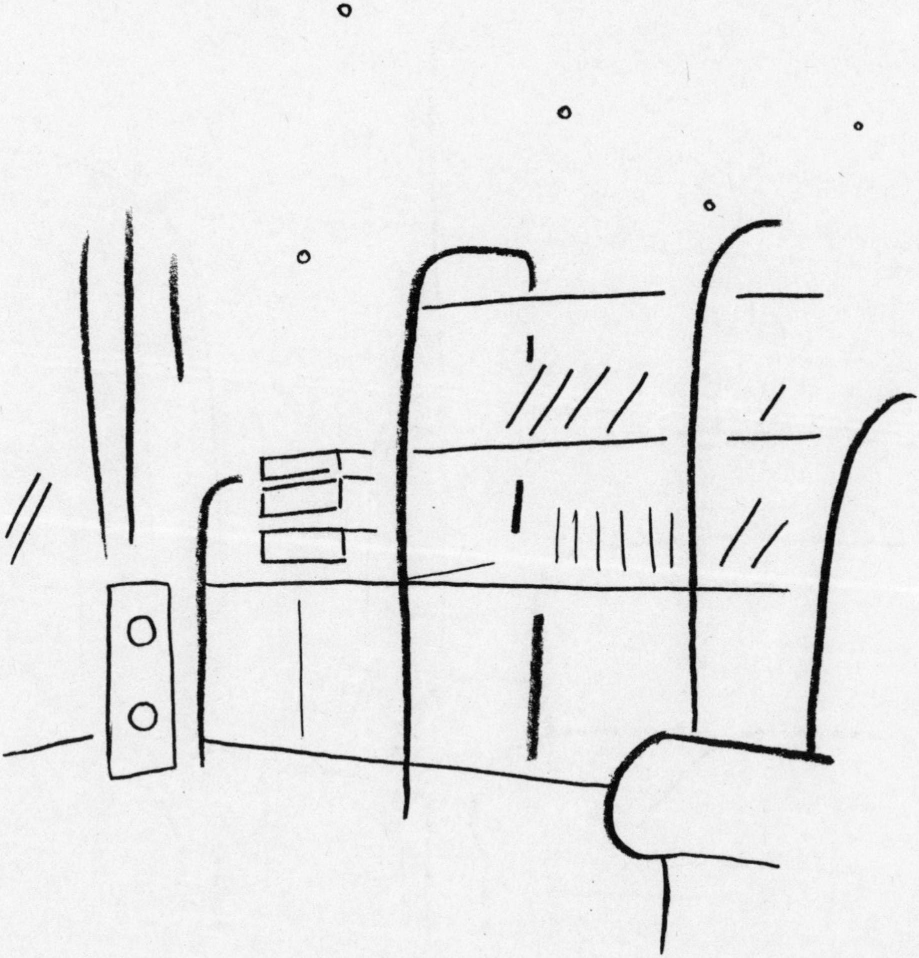

IT WAS TWO WEEKS BEFORE I LEFT HOME

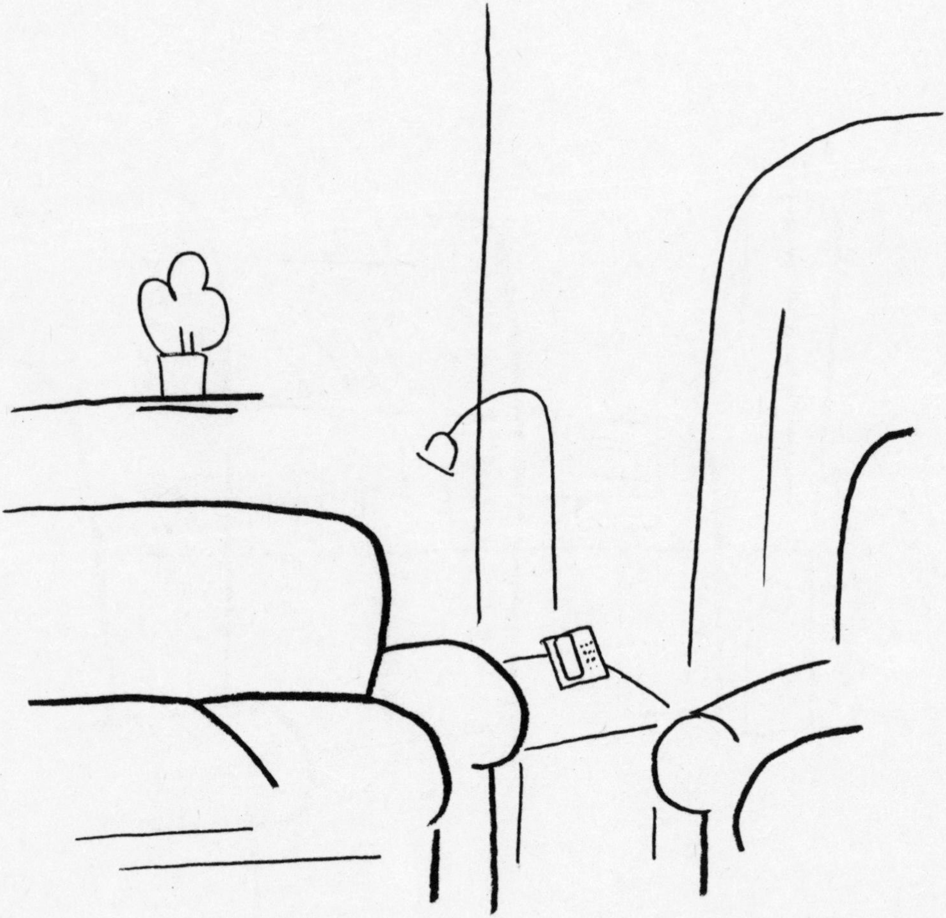

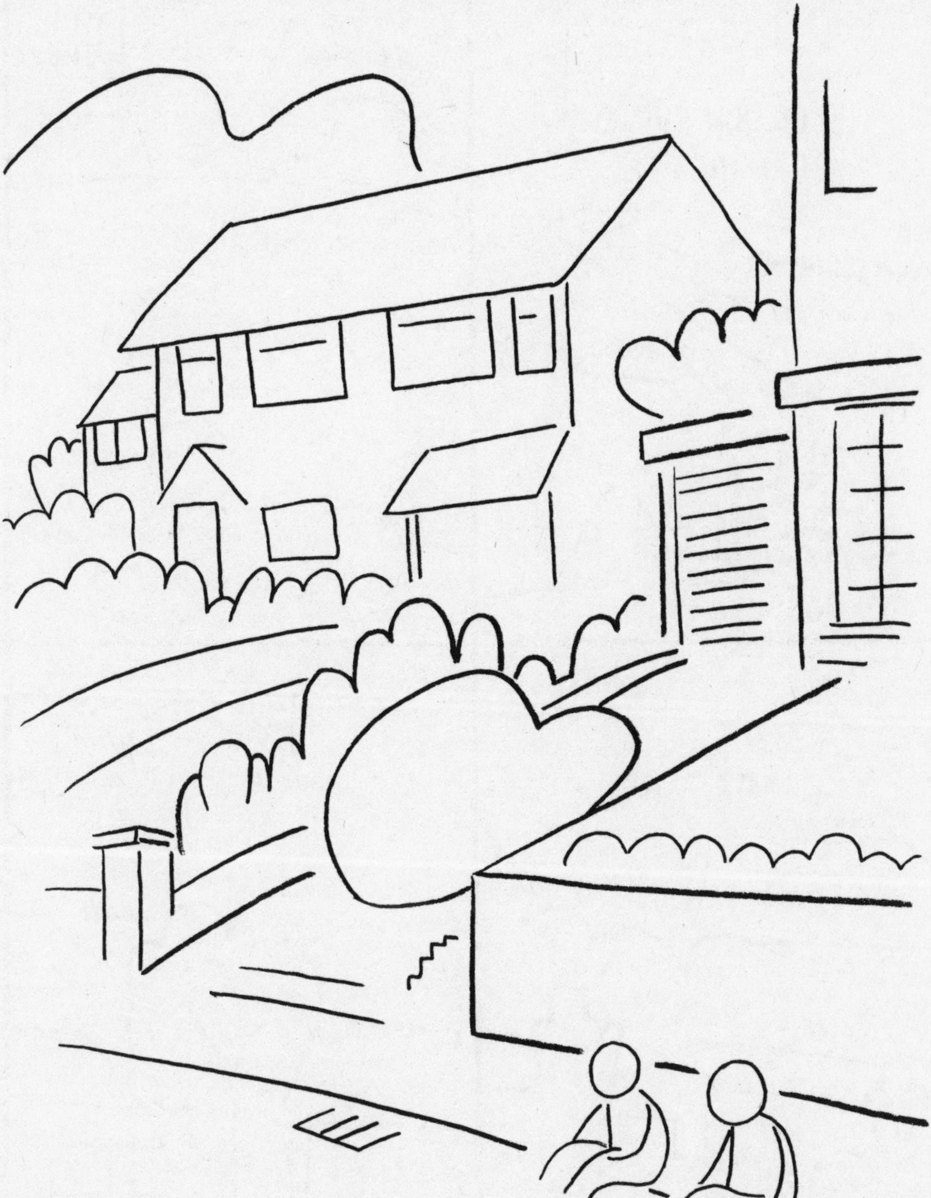

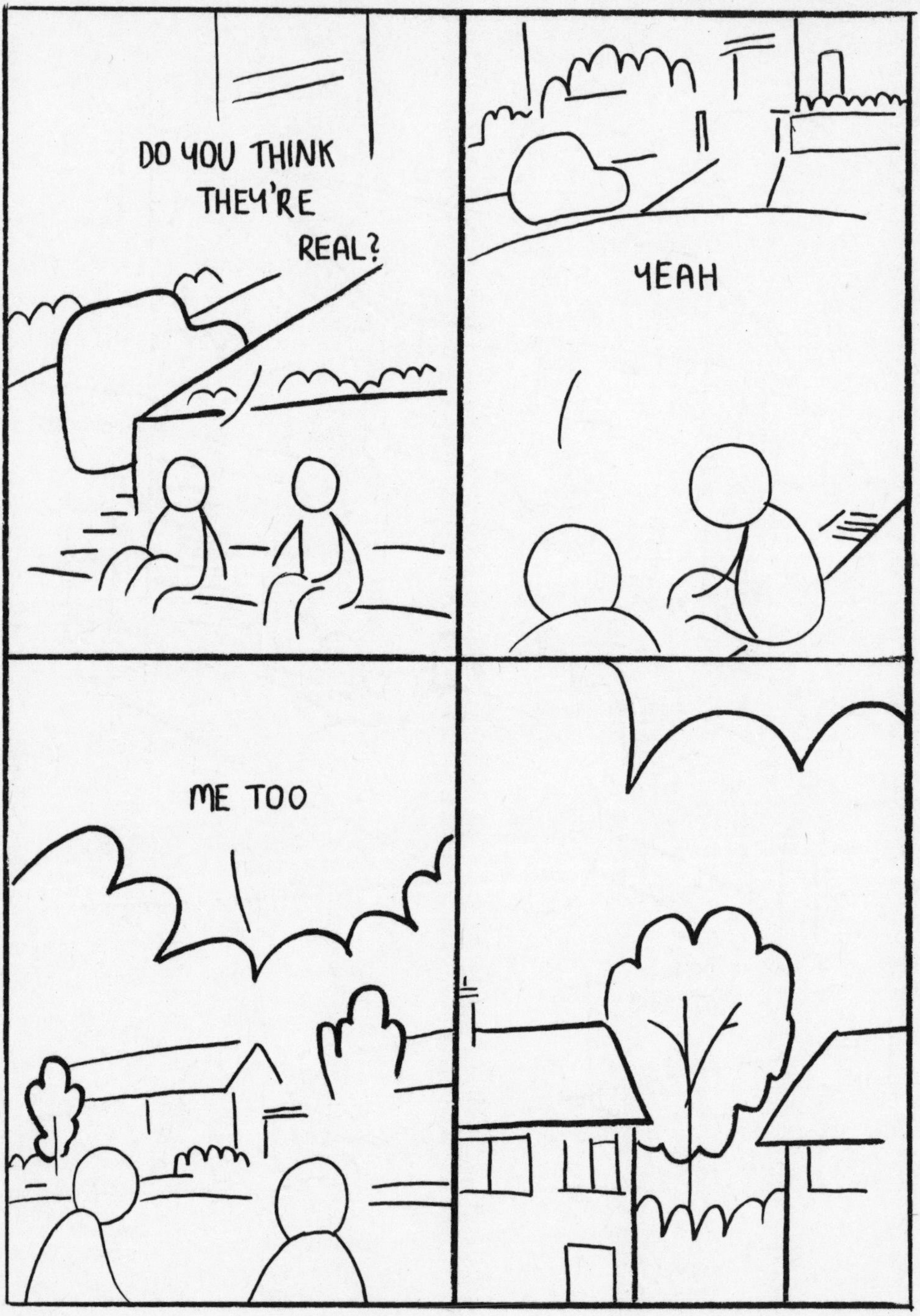
DO YOU THINK THEY'RE REAL?
YEAH
ME TOO

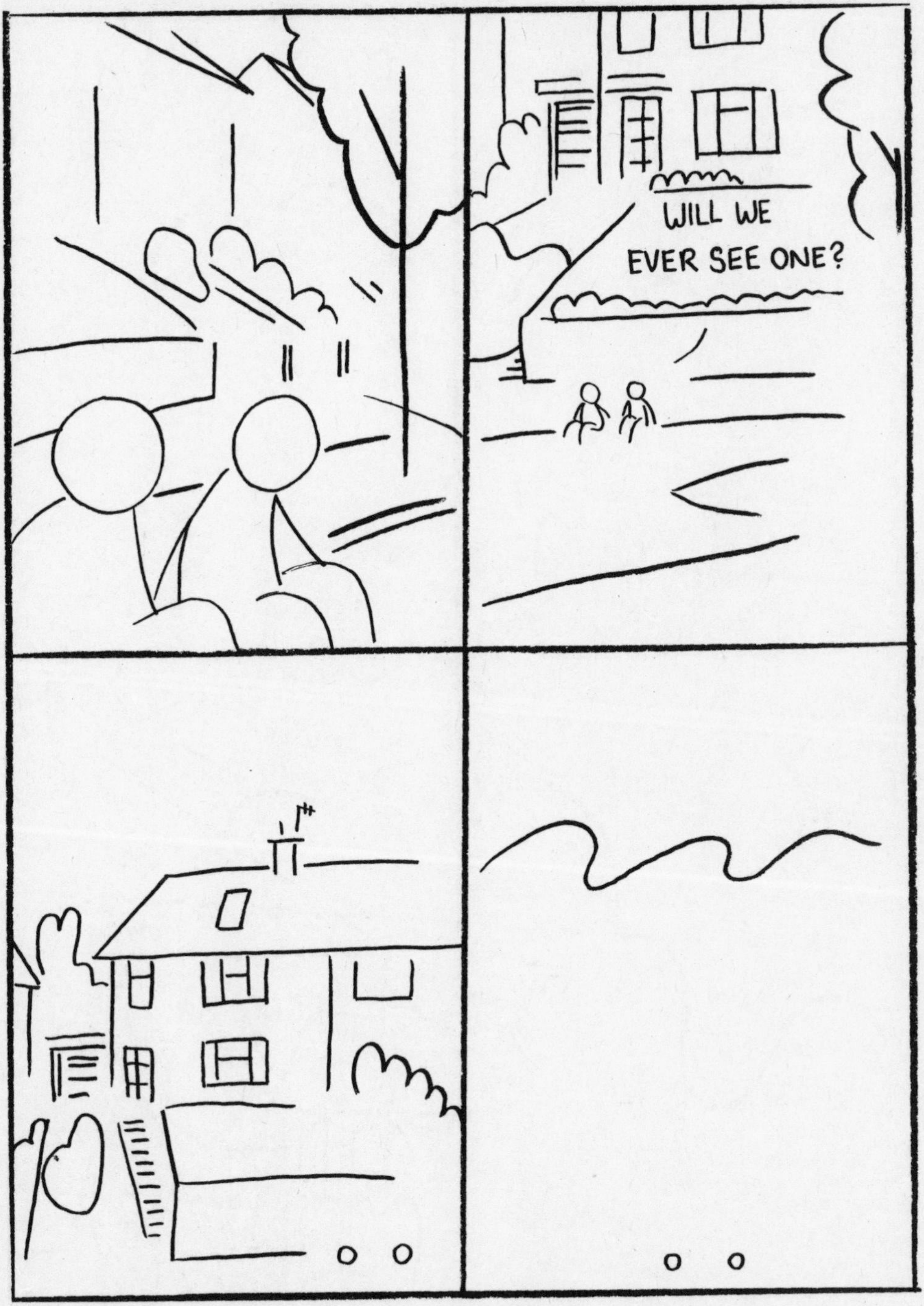
WILL WE
EVER SEE ONE?

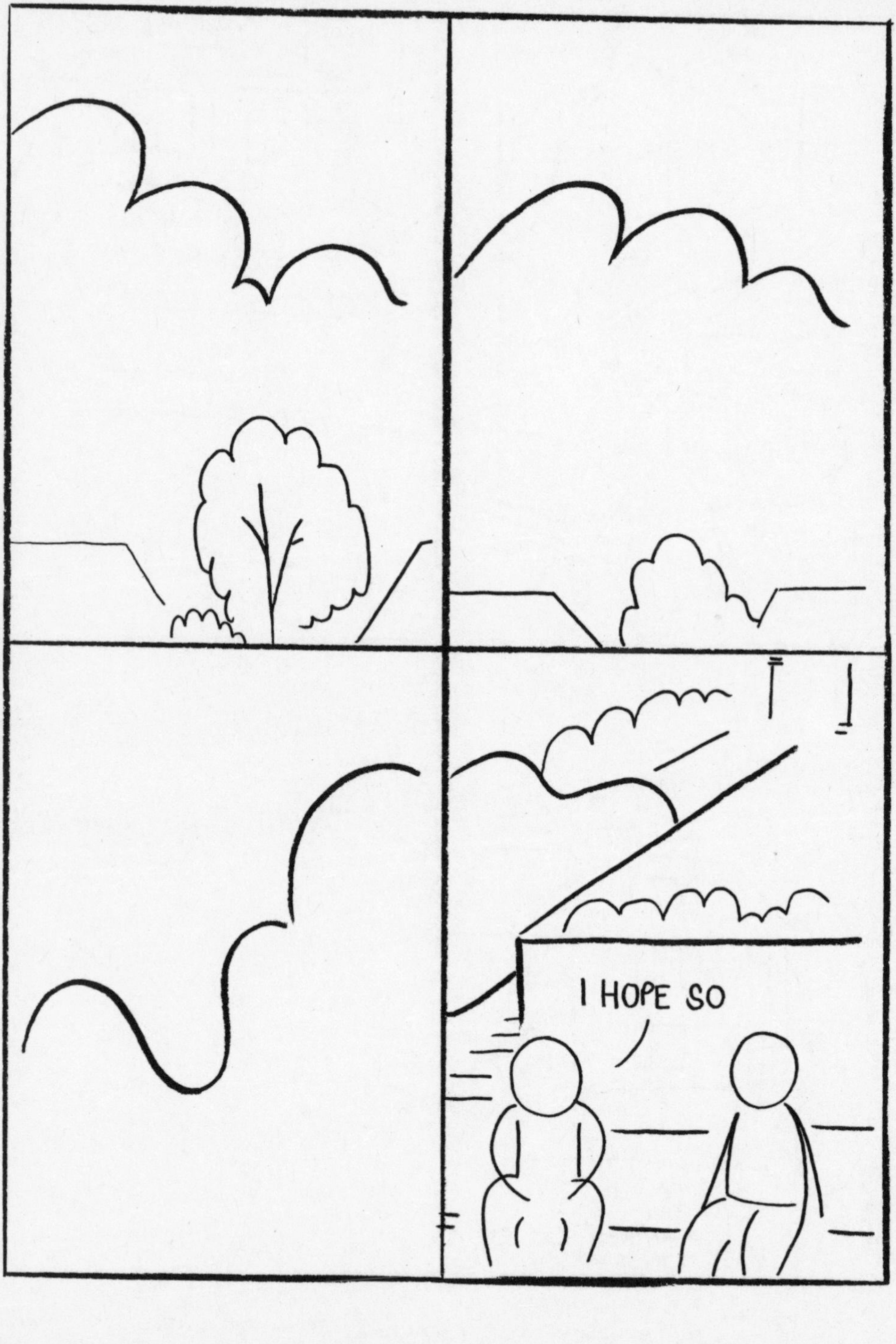
I HOPE SO

Thanks to (our) Ali, Andy, Anya, Beth, Chris, Claire, Haydn, Leith, Mac, Nat, Neel, Oli, Paul, Tom, my family, and (my) Ali for everything, then and now and forever. Thanks also to everyone who supported this book, and to Jordan and Tom K for making it happen. Thank you Marlow.